SHIFTING CULTIVATION IN INDIA

SHIFTING CULTIVATION IN INDIA

SACHCHIDANANDA

CONCEPT PUBLISHING COMPANY, NEW DELHI - 110059

Part I & Part II of this book were originally published in Vol. 2 & 3 of "Swidden Cultivation in Asia" by the UNESCO. The views expressed in the book, however, are those of the author and the UNESCO does not bear any responsibility for them".

ISBN 81-7022-040-8

First Published 1989

Sachchidananda (*b*. 1926-

Published and Printed by
Ashok Kumar Mittal
Concept Publishing Company
A/15-16, Commercial Block, Mohan Garden,
NEW DELHI-110059

Phones : 25351460, 25351794
Fax : 091-11-25357103
E-mail : publishing@conceptpub.com

Preface

Shifting cultivation was one of the several research themes suggested by the national seminars organized in 1977 by the UNESCO office of the Regional Adviser for Social Science in Asia and the Pacific to promote interest among the social scientists in the study of environment. These seminars stressed the need to guard against leaning either on the environment or on the culture. It was realised that in such a state, there should be a fusion between the two concerns of culture and environment and this can only be done through an inter-disciplinary perspective. Towards the end of December 1978, a symposium on this theme was organised at Bhubaneshwar. The organisers of the symposium approached the UNESCO for collaboration. Later on, towards the middle of 1979, a meeting was held in Bangkok at the UNESCO Regional Office to define the scope of this study and identify researchable sub-themes in the light of specificities of different national situations in the five countries, viz., Philippines, Thailand, Malaysia, Indonesia and India. Efforts were also made to formulate a common methodology of research to ensure comparability and to evolve an agreed format for the presentation of country reports. The first part of the exercise was the content analysis of the existing literature on shifting cultivation in the five countries under study. The second part was to deal with the country profile of shifting cultivation and the last part envisaged a holistic study of a community engaged in Swidden cultivation.

I came to be associated with the research programme from the second stage. At the request of the UNESCO Regional Office, I took up the preparation of the country profile for India in 1981. In this I was ably assisted by Shri K. N. Pathak, then one of the Research Fellows in the Sociology Division of our Institute. This was followed by the stage III of the study which was conducted in Arunachal Pradesh in 1982-83. I am extremely grateful to Professor Yogesh Atal, Regional Social Science Adviser in Asia and the Pacific, for giving me an opportunity to be associated with this study which was both thrilling and rewarding. The persuit of the holistic study took me to Arunachal Pradesh, the traditional home of shifting cultivation. It is the only part of India where the bulk of the cultivable land is under Swiddening. The study would not have been possible without the active help and co-operation from the Government of Arunachal Pradesh. The Director of Research, Dr. Parul Dutt, was not only extremely kind but accompanied me during my tours to the enchanting hills and dales of his area and made available to me his vast store of knowledge on the land and people in the areas of study.

The material incorporated in this book has been printed by UNESCO in Volumes II and III of the study entitled "Swidden Cultivation in Asia". Since this book is not readily available, Dr. Atal agreed to my suggestion to publish the Indian material in a composite volume so that it can be more easily accessible to Indian readers. The UNESCO headquarters on the recommendation of Dr. Atal gave me permission to this effect.

This study might not have seen the light of day without the active interest of Shri Naurang Rai of Concept Publishing Company, New Delhi who agreed to publish this in such a short time. I am indeed grateful to him for this.

Sachchidananda

A. N. Sinha Institute of Social Studies
PATNA

Introduction[1]

The total area within the world's tropics is estimated at 46 million sq. kilometers, 41.54 per cent of which is covered by forests. The tropical forests are nearly half of the total forested area of the world. The countries of Asia falling in the tropical category have 55 per cent of the total population living in forest areas. The five countries covered in the research programme of which the present study is a part relate to 500 million people inhabiting 127.9 million hectares of tropical humid forest areas. Their interactions with the forests have shaped their life style and also influenced the forest eco-system in a variety of ways.

The forest eco-system has productive, regulative and protective functions. These functions can acquire utility value for man and become functions of the cultural eco-system. The more important of these functions are protective, regulative and productive. The protective functions include social protection by absorption and deflection of radiation, precipitation and wind; conservation of humidity and carbon dioxide by decreasing wind velocity, sheltering and providing the required conditions for plant and animal species. The regulative functions include absorption, storage and release to Co_2, O_2 and mineral elements, absorption of aerosols and sound, absorption, storage and release of water and absorption and transformation and radiant thermal energy. The productivity functions include sufficient

1. * This is largely based on the Introduction to Vols. I and II of the book, *Swidden Cultivation in Asia*.

storage of energy utilizable forms; self-regulating and regenerating processes of wood, bark, fruit and leaf production and production of a wide array of chemical compounds such as resin alcaloids, essential oils, latex, etc.

These functions may be utilized by man for sheltering agricultural crops against wind, cold, rain; conserving soil and water and shielding man against nuisances like noise, smells, fumes, etc. It can lead man to improvement of atmospheric conditions in residential and recreational areas and improvement of temperature regimes in residential areas. It also results in the supply of a wide array of raw materials to meet man's growing demands, can provide employment and lead to creation of wealth.

Because of man-nature interaction in the tropical forest, the vegetative cover has been greatly modified and this has become a concern for ecologists. Logging, swiddening and agricultural development in the forest area have disturbed the eco-system. With the rising population and increasing mastery of man over nature, the tropical humidity forest areas are being rapidly reduced. The eco-system has been influenced by the use of fire by people practising swidden cultivation.

Swidden cultivation--socalled slash and burn or shifting cultivation--is still practised in many parts of the world by several ethnic groups and tribal communities. Swiddeners are usually identified as hill tribes or mountain people. Shifting cultivation is considered as a primitive form of agriculture and Swiddeners are regarded as backward, surving on subsistence economy.

Swiddeners have been a popular subject of anthropological research but they have never been studied in an integrated or inter-disciplinary manner so as to get a total picture of swiddening, of the life of swiddeners themselves, and of the relationship with the world outside. The studies carried out have been largely unidimensional and descriptive in nature and have therefore failed in analysing the dynamics of swidden cultivation and portraying its role in establishing the culture of its practitioners. Despite a long trend of research on swidden cultivation in anthropology, the existing literature does not have answers for the new questions raised today. Although excluded from the main current of civilisation and living high up in the mountains, the swiddeners cannot possibly be excluded from the process of development. Directly or indirectly the swiddeners are also drawn into the process and are under a continuous and systematic pressure to give up their age-old method of life and adopt modern style of life. The development may appear to be desirable but it is also a painful process.

Shifting cultivation has been much discussed not only by anthropologists but also by agricultural scientists. Anthropologists study this as an important element of primitive life and describe the various cultural patterns associated with it. More recently, the subject has attracted attention of ecologists. Instead of holding extreme positions favouring either culture or environment, the present trend is to view these as a part of interaction system and also see the problem in a symbiotic frame of reference. In the process the term swidden has been revived to replace the earlier prevalent term 'Shifting Cultivation' which connotes nomadic character of swiddeners. Some of these people live in permanent settled villages and make repeated cyclical use of some fields over a large area; others live in temporary villages which are abandoned as the fields became exhausted after a few years or few cycles of cultivation and fallow, some farmers combine or supplement their use of permanent irrigated fields for shifting cultivation specially where wet land is scarce.

Various typologies have been suggested for classification of shifting cultivation. Mahapatra suggested the typology based on the degree of dependence of this practice. The major types are (a) communities with exclusive dependence (b) communities with major dependence (c) communities with contingent dependence and (d) communities with marginal dependence.

The purpose of the present study is to provide a comprehensive over-view of swidden cultivation in India, followed by a case study from one community. The country profile is intended to bring in perspective geographic and environmental zones in which this kind of cultivation is practised, the demographic structure, economic system and social organisation of swiddeners and policy orientation of government towards swiddening and swiddeners. The profile begins with a brief introduction to the country in terms of its geographic and demographic diversity of culture, economic policy and developmental strategy. It then analyses the prevalence and extent of swidden cultivation in terms of area under this practice, some ethnic groups practising shifting cultivation, typology of swidden cultivation and brief cultural profiles of the communities concerned. This is followed by a historical review of the various measures taken by the Central and State Governments to improve the quality of life of the people practising this method and steps taken to control the practice of slash and burn cultivation. The present state of affairs in this field is analysed with a view to better understanding and appreciation of the problem.

Part II consists of a case study of a shifting cultivation community in Arunachal Pradesh, the traditional home of shifting cultivation. The community studied is the Wancho of Tirap district. This part of the study is based on intensive and comprehensive field work. It deals with the situation in five villages, focussing on the population and resource bases, the comparative productivity and various types of land use, the extent of subsistence and cash crop farming and other means of livelihood, household resource management, quality of life of the shifting cultivators, and the quality of environment in the village. Efforts made to control shifting cultivation in this particularly area have also been carefully analysed. Another community not far removed from that eco-system has also been studied to provide a contrasting picture from the point of view of responses of swiddeners to steps taken by the Government for their relocation on permanent agricultural fields.

In the case study an attempt has been made to analyse how the tribal communities engaged in this practice have altered under forces of socio-economic change. In most modern states, social change and development are seen as parts of the process of industrialisation and modernisation. Economically and technologically this change is regarded as a part of the industrialisation process and socially and culturally illustrative of the consequences of modernisation. The socio-economic change has naturally brought about the changes at the personal level particularly in the area of values and norms. The advent of cash economy in the swiddening sector together with the community's exposure to urban culture has enforced the dependency of rural population on the urban sectors. The swiddening community may be viewed as a 'satellite' or 'periphery' in relation to the urban complexes. The export oriented markets affects the swidden's production activity.

An effort has been made to see the entire problem through emic perspective, i.e., the perspective of the tribal himself who lives in that culture. Steps sought by the modernisers of the problem-that are non-existent for the tribals-are, therefore, irrelevant or non-applicable to the tribal. In most cases he has not been provided with the alternative ways of making a living.

The four basic questions tried to be answered in the present study are as follows:

1. Is shifting cultivation a practice peculiar only to primitive tribes;
2. Is shifting cultivation viewed as an economic activity or does it need to be studied in a specific historical and socio-political context? It has sometimes been held as a product of heirarchical societies which pushed and exploited small tribal communities. A situation has been created through which the tribal has become refugee in his own habitat;
3. Is shifting cultivation really un-economical? Does it destroy the environment? Some of the environmental specialists take the stand that in the kind of environment in which shifting cultivation is practised, it is the most rational form of cultivation as no other form of cultivation is possible nor economical;
4. Can there be a positive policy towards shifting cultivation rather than condemning it as bad? Will it not be advisable to improve the methodology of shifting cultivation so that the yield is increased and damage done to the environment caused by it is minimised? It is argued that any situation of man-environment interaction is physically exploitative and some damage to the environment is inevitable, no matter what form of agriculture people practise. Therefore, there is no reason to single out only this form of environmental exploitation for wholesale condemnation.

Contents

Part One

INDIA

Chapter One

PERSPECTIVES OF SWIDDEN CULTIVATION

Swidden cultivation occupies a distinct place in the tribal economy. It constitutes a vital part of the socio-economic network of tribal life. Hence for a proper analysis of the socio economic life of the tribals the analysis of shifting cultivation appears to be a prerequisite. According to Pelzer (1958),

> Shifting field agriculture may be defined as an agricultural system which is characterized by a rotation of fields rather than of crops, by short period of cropping (one to three years) alternating with long fallow periods (up to twenty and more years, but often as short as six to eight years) and by clearing by means of slash and burn.

As Conklin (1957) explains,

> Shifting Cultivation implies an aimless, unplanned, nomadic movement or an abrupt change in location, either of which may refer to the cropping areas, the agriculturists, or both. Aside from being ambiguous and in many cases inaccurate, these implications do not focus attention on the two most widely shared characteristic of these various system; *firing and fallowing.*

However, making it more precise in a recent minimal definition, Conklin (1961) described shifting cultivation as 'any agricultural system in which fields are cleared by firing and are cropped discontinuously'.

Basic features of shifting cultivation

The minimal definition of shifting cultivation reflects its real value. However, a single definition does not appear to be wide enough to touch upon all its essential aspects. Firing and discontinuous cropping by shifting of the plot are two gross morphological criteria which could be used as most significant and useful diagonistic elements in the analysis of shifting cultivation. Nevertheless, many variations are found in the basic elements as well as in the other critically important phases of the crop production cycle. Hence, to make a comprehensive analysis of the patterns of swiddening as practised by the peoples over different parts of the tropics, it is imperative that the following features and qualitative elements should be taken into account:

1. practised chiefly by simpler cultures or small total populations but occasionally used by almost anyone to whom the cropping system appears expedient;

2. human labour chiefly operative, using a few handtools primarily, but powertools are used occasionally;

3. labour pattern frequently co-operative, but involving many variations in working group structure;

4. clearing of fields primarily by felling, cutting, slashing and burning, and using fire to dispose of vegetative debris after drying (in special situations fire may not be used);

5. frequent shifting of cropped fields, normally in some kind of sequence in land control, resting in special social groupings under customary law, but sometimes occuring under other legal institutions of land control;

6. many different systems in crop planting in given fields but both multiple cropping and specialized cropping present;

7. use of annual and short-term food crops predominant, but important use of long-term shrub and tree crops is common;

8. use of crops primarily for subsistence but exchange patterns may reach total sale of whole product;

9. use of permanent dooryard, village near homestead garden frequent among groups using permanent or near permanent settlement sites;

10. fields per acre and per man-hour normally compare with those of permanent field agriculture within regions in which comparision is properly made but yields are often below those of mechanically-powered permanent-field agriculture;

11. small annual cropped area per capita but comparable to that of the other non-powered sedentary cropping systems;

12. use of vegetative cover as soil conditioner and source of plant nutrient for cropping cycle;

13. when system is efficiently operated, soil erosion not greater than soil erosion under other systems that are being efficiently operated;

14. soil depletion not more serious than that under other systems of agriculture when operated efficiently;

15. details of practice vary greatly depending upon the physical environment and the cultural milieu;

16. transiency of residence common but not universal, with many patterns of residence according to the evolutionary level or detailed system employed and preference of culture group;

17. operative chiefly in the regions where more technologically advanced systems of agriculture have not become economically or culturally possible or in regions where the land has not yet been appropriated by people with greater political or cultural power;

18. destructive of natural resources only when operated inefficiently and not more inherently destructive than other systems of agriculture when these are operated inefficiently;

19. a residual system of agriculture largely replaced by other systems except where retention or practice is expedient.

It is obvious that the above gross characteristics do not conform to the list of features frequently set down as characteristic of shifting cultivation.

Numerous studies on Swidden or shifting cultivation in India have been conducted by various institutions and individual researchers. However, most of the studies have been conducted as part of ethnographic studies of tribes. Only a few studies present a comparative estimate of different states or regions making it difficult to work on a country profile of Swidden cultivator societies. The first major work of comparative nature is that of D.C. Kaith. He made a thorough statewise study of the swidden cultivator tribes His study provides a statistical analysis of the number of households in relation to total population of the swidden cultivators, the area under swidden cultivation and the crops grown in this pattern. The data on the area cut annually for swidden and the district-wise analysis enables an assessment to be made of the enormity of the situation. But since 1956-1957 when Kaith did his study, a number of changes have taken place not only in the mode of living of the swidden cultivator tribes and their economic system, but also in state boundaries.

Another study covering different states and regions was by B.K. Roy Burman and P.S. Sharma (1970) done in the 1960s. Besides other things the study presents a breakup of tribes practising swidden cultivation by states. One more work in the 1960s was by Sardendu Bose who made an in-depth study of the socio-economic interrelations among the swidden cultivator tribes of Abujhmar Hills, Keonjhar Hills and Lushai Hills. In his work, Bose (1967) also examined the carrying capacity of land in these three regions and thus provided a background for changes to be brought about. The work of Dar (1970) is again based on the figures of the 1960s. This study covers the swidden cultivators of Northeast and South India. Dar has traced the statewise population depending on swidden cultivation and presented data about the land available per person for swidden cultivation. This provides a broader perception of the economic basis of swidden cultivation. On the basis of facts and figures available therein, Dar evaluated the success of the *jhum* control measures and that of the alternative measures evolved. A similar study by Pal (1980), based on the figures of the 1960s, presented the figures on the population of swidden cultivators in relation to the total population of agricultural tribes and analysed the agricultural pattern in relation to the social system.

There was no study in the 1970s which could provide an all-India estimate of swidden cultivator societies corresponding to the increase in population and other socio-economic changes. The only inter-state study on swidden cultivator tribes in the 1970s covers only Northeastern India (Saikia and Kalita 1979). However, there have been a number of studies highlighting the socio-economic features of a particular region or particular tribes.

The study by Das (1945) on the Purum of Manipur provides an intimate view of the impact of the social and cultural milieu on the economy of the Purum in the first half of this century. Nag (1958), deals with the economic system of the Baiga at much length, and presents a comparative study on shifting cultivator economy in

Assam, Orissa, Madhya Pradesh, Tamilnadu and Andhra Pradesh. Mahapatra (1953, 1965, 1979), Patnaik (1977) and Mandal (1977), Mahapatra and Kiranbala (1972-73), and Mahapatra (1969-1970, 1976), give details about some swidden communities in Orissa. Of the studies conducted on central India the important ones are those by Mathur (1976), Patel (1968) and Jay (1970, 1974). Vidyarthi (1963) made an in-depth study of shifting cultivation among the Maler.

The work of Haimendorf (1945) on Hill Reddis examines the economy of that society in the light of historical experience. The work of Raju (1971) on Jatapu examines the impact of developmental measures taken for the economic upliftment of the shifting cultivator tribe. The study of Koya by Tyler (1974) is thorough and examines the various facets of the Koya shifting cultivation. Other such exclusive studies covering tribes of South India are by Morab (1977) on the Soliga and by Sastry (1977) on other tribes of Karnataka. In *New deal for tribal India,* Elwin (1963) makes a strong plea for scientific shifting cultivation.

Some efforts have recently been made towards the study of shifting cultivation in India. Mahapatra (1979) has divided India into two zones for the analysis of shifting cultivation. The first is central India comprising Madhya Pradesh and Orissa and the second, North-east India comprising the states of Assam, Nagaland, Meghalaya, Manipur and Union Territory of Mizoram and Arunachal Pradesh. He finds only four tribes of Madhya Pradesh presently practising shifting cultivation. In Orissa about one sixth of the total land of the state involving about a million people is under this practice. No actual estimate has been found about the rest of the country. On the basis of his experience, Mahapatra formulates two main patterns of shifting cultivation, the central and North Eastern. On the basis of his observations Mahapatra (1979) formulates four major categories of shifting cultivators in terms of the degree of their dependence on swidden cultivation. The first category is that of *exclusive dependence.* This includes such cultivator tribes of which about three fourths or more households are dependent on swidden. The cultivators under this category are landless and immigrant and their households are exclusively dependent on swidden. The second category is that of *major dependence.* This includes tribes in which 50-74 per cent depend almost wholly on swidden cultivation while the rest of such a tribe may take up other modes of agricultural production. In this category the income from swidden is supplemented through mining or wage labour, tea plantation labour or other subsidiary sources of income. The third category is that of *contingent dependence,* which includes such tribes where almost all households of resettled, displaced or disinherited or transplanted village communities may practise swidden for two to three years as a contingent phase emerging out of some governmental action of resettlement or colonization. The fourth category is that of *marginal dependence.* It includes cultivators whose income by swidden does not constitute more than 25 per cent of the total income from all the sources.

These studies, however, do not give any idea of the extent of the area under shifting cultivation and the total population involved throughout the country. There is no information about the impact of recent measures to wean the tribals away from this system or the number of people who have been relocated on permanent fields. The area covered in the different studies by different authors varies widely. While conducting the study of shifting cultivators, some areas or tribes covered in the previous studies are excluded whereas some new ones are added. Hence, it is not possible to measure the change taking place over a period of time. Sometimes data presented about a particular tribe or region are contradictory. For instance, the extent of area covered under shifting cultivation in Madhya Pradesh in 1961 is shown as 947,680 acres (379,072 hectares) by Roy Burman and Sharma (1970) whereas Mahapatra puts it to be only 44,000 acres (17,600 hectares). This gross difference cannot be explained.

The two all-India estimates presented by D.C. Kaith in 1956 and Roy Burman and Sharma in 1970 appear to be largely identical. Virtually no change is noted to have taken place in the extent of land and population involved in shifting cultivation in 1950s and 1960s. It seems that both the estimates originate from the same source though they claim relevance for different points of time.

There are hardly any figures about the land and population involved in shifting cultivation or per capita availability of swidden land in the 1970s. However, the study by Saikia and Kalita (1979) provides such information for the Northeastern States. A large number of states mentioned in that study are carved out of Assam. Thus, a comparative study of even these states is not possible.

The study of Swidden cultivation in India involves the analysis of the topography of the country in relation to the existing socio-economic system. The country may be divided into three broadly defined physiographic units: (1) the Himalayas and the associated mountain chains; (2) the Ganga-Brahmaputra plain; and (3) the Deccan plateau. The Himalayas comprise a series of parallel mountain ranges characterized by topographic complexity of a high order. It stretches thousands of miles from west to east. The southern plateau is an old mass of the earth's crust worn down by continuous erosion. It is characterized by plateau surfaces, broken by striking ridges, valleys and hill ranges. In between the two physiographic units lies the Ganga-Brahmaputra plain. It is full of riverine deposits. The filling has been done so uniformly that the plain gives an impression of a flat surface. It is largely in the hills of eastern India and in the central Indian hills and plateaux that swidden cultivation is found.

Till 1921, the population of the country was alternately increasing and decreasing. The rise in population was rather halting and meagre. The year 1921 is recorded as a great divide in the demographic history of India. After 1921, with improved transport and means of communication, movement of food became easier during famines, and public health measures prepared the way for a reduction in the number of deaths. From that year there has been a steady growth in population. During 1921 to 1951, the rise in population was at the rate of 1.3 per cent per annum. In the decade 1961 to 1971 the rate of increase was 2.4 per cent per annum. This is on account of a vast decline in the death rate accompanied by an insignificant fall in birth rate. The total population of the country in 1971 was recorded as 547.9 million. The provisional population figures for 1981 were 683.8 million.

In India 80 per cent of the population live in villages. The density of population was 178 persons per square kilometre according to the 1971 count. The most densely populated areas are Kerala, the Ganga-Jamuna plains, and West Bengal. In some agricultural districts in North Bihar and in Kerala the density rises above 600 persons per square kilometre. Only 20 per cent of the population live in urban areas. There are nearly 150 cities with more than 100,000 people. There are also nine metropolitan centres which have a population of one million or more. These 160 cities accounted for 56 per cent of the total urban population in the country. This trend towards growing urbanization is indicative of great pressure on land. The capacity of agriculture to absorb more people seems to have reached a point of saturation.

The country is so vast that there is enormous diversity of physical types, language, religion and caste. Distinct culture areas can be marked out in the country. However, the social ethos of India reflects a high degree of unity in diversity. The large geographical spread of the country provides fertile ground for the germination and flowering of regional diversities in the social environment. The differentiation in the natural landscapes is attributed to the emergence of different forms and patterns of man-nature interactions in the different regions of India. The food the people eat, the clothes they wear, the houses they live in, the economic activities they carry out, the languages and dialects they speak, the festivals they organize, the myths and legends which embody their emotional responses, all show great variety. The transhumant Gujjar herdsmen in the Pir Panjal, the Moplah fishermen of Malabar, the Maratha peasants of the block cotton soil belt, the *jhum* cultivators of the humid north-east, and the industrial workers in the various urban centres have all been coming to terms with their specific ecosystems.

The differing sources of waves of immigration in the sub-continent from the surrounding countries is a process spread over thousands of years. The different routes of dispersal of these into the various corners of the country and the consequent concentration of diverse ethnic elements in the different regions has created a social mosaic with distinct regional concentrations.

The unique feature of the social geography of India is not the extent of its plurality but the fact that social diversity has been based on, and is sustained by, underlying unity which has evolved over time. In spite of the differences in natural environments of various regions, the monsoonal rhythm of the seasons provides a strong element of uniformity. The alternation of dry and wet seasons and the concentration of life-giving rains in a few months in a year is by and large an all-India phenomenon. The music and the fragrance produced by raindrops falling on parched thirsty earth generates intense emotional response among people almost everywhere in India and it is on this that their rain-fed subsistence agriculture and the village community is based.

The horizontal spread of cultural and socio-economic attributes from different parts of the country and the ever-growing give-and-take through interregional contacts and exchanges have generated a process of cultural fusion. Foremost of all these integrative forces was the spread of Vedic and Puranic traditions all over the country. This horizontal spread performed the unifying role, and in the process, these great traditions developed the capacity to assimilate elements of regional traditions and thereby enriching and transforming itself.

The development of inter-regional economic linkages and the emergence of a national home market also played an important role in unifying the country. The networks of railways and other means of communication greatly facilitated the unification process. The rural-urban migration stream brought together into urban agglomeration people who spoke different languages and dialects and professed different faiths but were citizens of an emergent India.

The ethnic composition of the country is reflected in the concentration of the Mediterraneans in the south, the Nordics in the north and north-west, and Tibeto-Mongoloids in the Himalayan region and the north-eastern valleys. The bulk of the tribal population in the belt of middle India is, however, composed of the Proto-australoids. There is a sprinkling of Negrito elements in Kerala and in a few communities in Gujrat and also in the Andaman Islands.

The vast majority of the Indian population follows Hinduism. The Muslims form nearly 12 per cent of the total population. The Sikhs and the Christians account for a much smaller percentage. Other religions are Buddhism and Zoroastrianism. However, the most important feature of the Indian social system is caste. It continues to exert tremendous influence on the social life of India. Originally rooted in Hinduism, its influence is also found among Muslims, Sikhs, and Christians. As a result of conversion, a person may lose his religion in India but he hardly ever loses his caste. In this connection, the existence of social and economically deprived caste groups known as the scheduled castes may be noted. Their concentration reflects, in important ways, the incidence of poverty within the regional structure and indicates a varying magnitude and breadth of socio-economic exploitation in different regions of the country.

From the point of view of language, India is marked by a great deal of linguistic diversity. Out of the 187 languages spoken in India 23 are spoken by as many as 97 per cent of the population. The languages can be divided broadly into four families: (1) the Dravidian languages of the south; (2) the Indo-Aryan languages of the north and north-west; (3) the Mon Khmer and the Tibeto-Burman languages of the north-east and the Himalayan region; and (4) the Austric language family in the Aravali-Vindhya-Chotanagpur complex. Hindi accounts for the largest number of speakers in the country. There are 13 other languages which have been recognized as regional languages in different parts of the country.

India is basically an agricultural country from which 70 per cent of its people derive their livelihood. Ever since independence, agricultural production has been growing steadily. More and more areas of the country have been brought under cultivation with increasing irrigation facilities. The dependence on monsoon rain has been reduced to some extent and in many areas a second and a third crop is also grown.

Industrial development has taken place at a fast pace since independence and India now figures as one of the industrialized countries of the world. New areas have been opened up with new rail routes and national highways. A series of five-year plans have accelerated the pace of development. Besides agricultural and industrial development, significant strides have been made in rural development. New strategies have been evolved to see that the benefits of development reach the weaker sections of the community, namely the scheduled tribes and the scheduled castes, the rural artisans, the landless labourers, and women. Integrated rural development programmes have been drawn up to provide for the all-round development of the people. In areas where the scheduled tribes are concentrated, integrated tribal development projects have also been initiated. These are trying to raise the quality of life of the tribal peoples, who hitherto had largely remained cut off from the general development in the region.

Chapter Two

LAND, AND THE PEOPLE INVOLVED

In the larger part of Northeastern India the term frequently used for shifting cultivation is *Jhum.* However, in many tribal communities of central and South India it bears different names. In Maghalaya it is known as *Bogma* among the Garos, *Lyngkhalum* or *Shyrti* among the Khasis, *Rit* among the Mikirs of Assam, *Tekonglu* among the Ao Nagas of Manipur, *Adiabik* among the Adis of Lushai Hills, *Hookuismong* among the Reangs of Tripura, *Lankapadsenad* by Koya, and *Remo, Dahi Kaman* or *Biringa* by the Bhuinyas of North Orissa, *Gudia, Bagda, Sarban Donger Chara* or *Podu* in Southern Orissa; as *Beonra* among the Birjhia and as *Kurwa* among the Maler of Chotanagpur, as *Bewar, Dahiya,* or *Penda* in Madhya Pradesh, and as *Podu* among the hill Reddis of Andhra Pradesh.

Over a large part of Northeastern India the chief characteristics of shifting cultivation, while having different local names are found to be the same. These are: (1) rotation of fields; (2) use of fire for clearing the land; (3) keeping the land fallow for regeneration for a number of years; (4) use of human labour as main input; (5) non-employment of draught animals; (6) non-use of the plough, but instead very crude and simple implements such as dibble sticks and scrapers, are used, and (7) all the crops being grown are mixed together. Furthermore, in most parts of Northeast India it is found that hunting and gathering is an important subsidiary occupation of the shifting cultivators (Saikia, 1976).

Land-man ratio

A thorough review of the tribal people practising shifting cultivation indicates that a considerable percentage of population is engaged in such practice. The following table shows the percentage of those engaged in shifting cultivation to the total tribesmen working as cultivators.

The above data reveal that the states most affected by shifting cultivation are Manipur, Tripura, Orissa, Assam, and Andhra Pradesh.

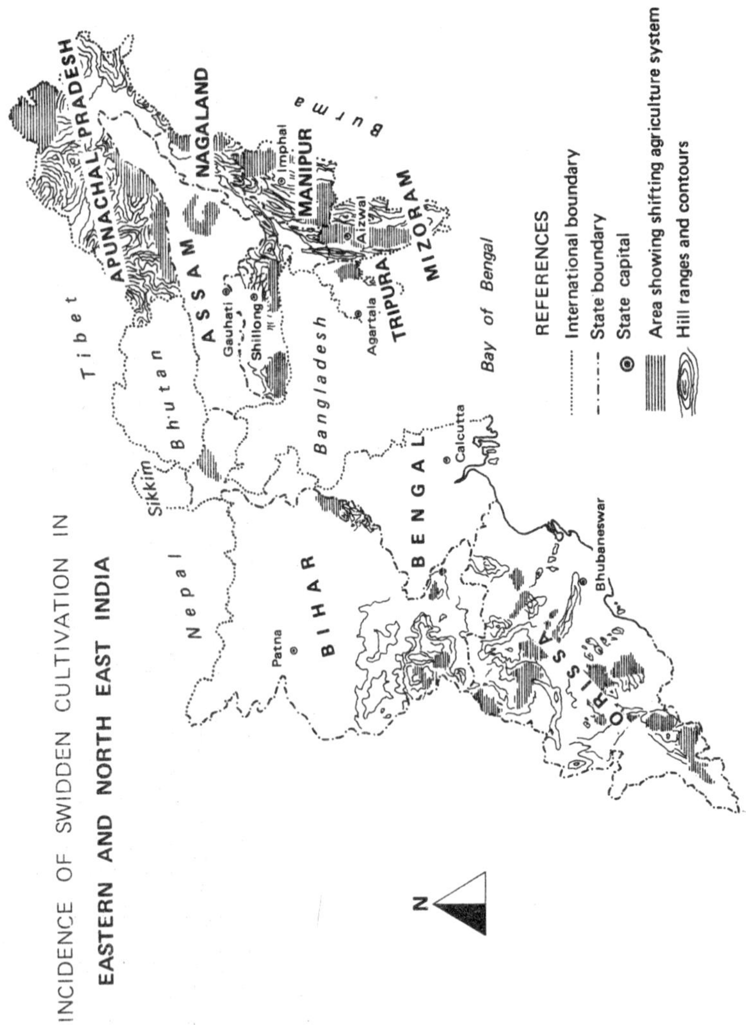

INCIDENCE OF SWIDDEN CULTIVATION IN
EASTERN AND NORTH EAST INDIA

Table 1. Shifting cultivators as percentage of total tribal population in various states.

State	*Percentage*
Assam	47
Manipur	73.5
Tripura	60
Orissa	66.6
Bihar	6
Madhya Pradesh	1
Maharashtra	1.6
Karnataka	32
Andhra Pradesh	51
Kerala	39
Tamil Nadu	2.6

Source: B.N. Pal, "Some economic aspects of tribal agriculture" in Vidyarthi and Sahay (ed) *Applied Anthropology and development in India,* Delhi, 1980, p. 117.

Table 2. Availability of land per capita in Selected States of India

State	*Available land per cultivator (acres)*
Assam	0.52
Manipur	0.29
Tripura	1.22
Orissa	0.43
Bihar	0.004
Madhya Pradesh	1.47
Maharashtra	2.89
Karnataka	0.18
Andhra Pradesh	0.48
Kerala	5.40
Madras (Tamil Nadu)	1.39

* *Source:* Pal, 1980, p. 118.

The commissioner for scheduled castes and scheduled tribes in his report for 1961 calculated the per-cultivator availability of land for some states as follows:

This shows that the availability of land per cultivator is very uneconomical and unable to provide a subsistence living for a single family.

Geophysical features

Shifting cultivation is practised in India in all the humid regions of Southern and Southeastern India, from the tidal coasts to upper limits of crop growth in the higher mountains. Only India and West Pakistan contain areas too arid for the normal practice of shifting cultivation. Parts of Deccan and the Northwest of India lie outside the zone of active shifting cultivation.

The tropical regions with a mean temperature of approximately 18.3°C and a minimum of 24 inches (610 mm) of rainfall per annum and with a thin population have been found to be favourable for swidden cultivation (Saikia, 1979).

The system of swidden cultivation is regarded as the first stage of purposeful use of soil for crop production and is still prevalent among most of the hill tribes of Northeast India and some of the tribes of central and Southeast India.

Ecologically the main factors responsible for swidden cultivation in these tropical regions are the rapid exhaustion of soil fertility and the low capability of soils to retain plant nutrients. The Food and Agriculture Organization of the United Nations (FAO) explains the situation as follows:

> These difficulties can be split into several factors – low absorptive capacity for exchangable bases of the soil's clays fractions, the tendency of these clays to immobilize phosphates, the heavy percolation rate of tropical rain through generally very porous soils and the resulting leaching of plant nutrients, the rapid destruction of organic matter by bacterial action under conditions of high temperatures and so on (FAO, 1957).

For an analysis of the pattern of swidden cultivation and its related aspects and for the critical evaluation of this mode of cultivation in the ethnography of tribal society or of a particular tribe, its impact on the concerned population and on the national economy, it is imperative that a study of tribal India be made in terms of geographical and demographic divisions. For this purpose, we may divide India into three main regions inhabited by tribal populations.

1. *North and north-eastern region* — The area extends from the foothills of the Himalayas to the north-eastern hill areas of Nagaland, Garo hills, Khasi hills and Mizo hills, hill regions of Orissa, and the hills of Chotanagpur. The State and Union Territories covered in this region are Arunanachal Pradesh, Assam, Manipur, Meghalaya, Mizoram, Nagaland and Tripura, West Bengal, Orissa, and Bihar. The principal tribes living in these areas are Lepcha, Meeh, Kachai, Miri, Mikir, Garo, Khasi, Naga, Kuki, Abor, Adi, Chakmo, Mogs, Noga, Mishmi, Apatani, Dafla, Lushai, Gallong, Noatia, Reang, Gadba, Juang, Maler.

In the north-eastern region swidden cultivation is prevalent among many of the Naga tribes, such as the Sema Naga, Konyak Naga; the Kuki tribes of Mizo hills; the Mikir and Modo group tribes of Assam and the Abor group of tribes, Dafla hill, Miri, Aka of Arunanchal Pradesh.

2. *Central and West India* — This region consists of mountainous regions of Vindhyas covering central Madhya Pradesh, Satpura mountain range covering southern Madhya Pradesh, and north-western Maharashtra and forest of Arawali covering southern Rajasthan and some parts of north-western Madhya Pradesh. This zone comprises the states of Uttar Pradesh, Madhya Pradesh, Gujrat, and Maharashtra. The principal tribes inhabiting this range are Saora, Salsor, Faria, Khond, Ho, Bhumij, Korwa, Gond, Bhil, Baiga, Muria, Maria of Madhya Pradesh, and Kalki, Katkari, Kumari Marahta, Maria Gond, Thakur and Wakkal of Maharashtra.

3. *Tribal region of the Deccan Plateau* — This region extends from across the Godavari River, covering the southern part of the river Krishna and includes all the mountainous region of the south such as Nallamalai Hills, Javadi Hills, Nilgiri Hills, Shevaroy Hills and Cardamom Hills. The states covered in this region are Karnataka, Andhra Pradesh, Kerala, and Tamil Nadu.

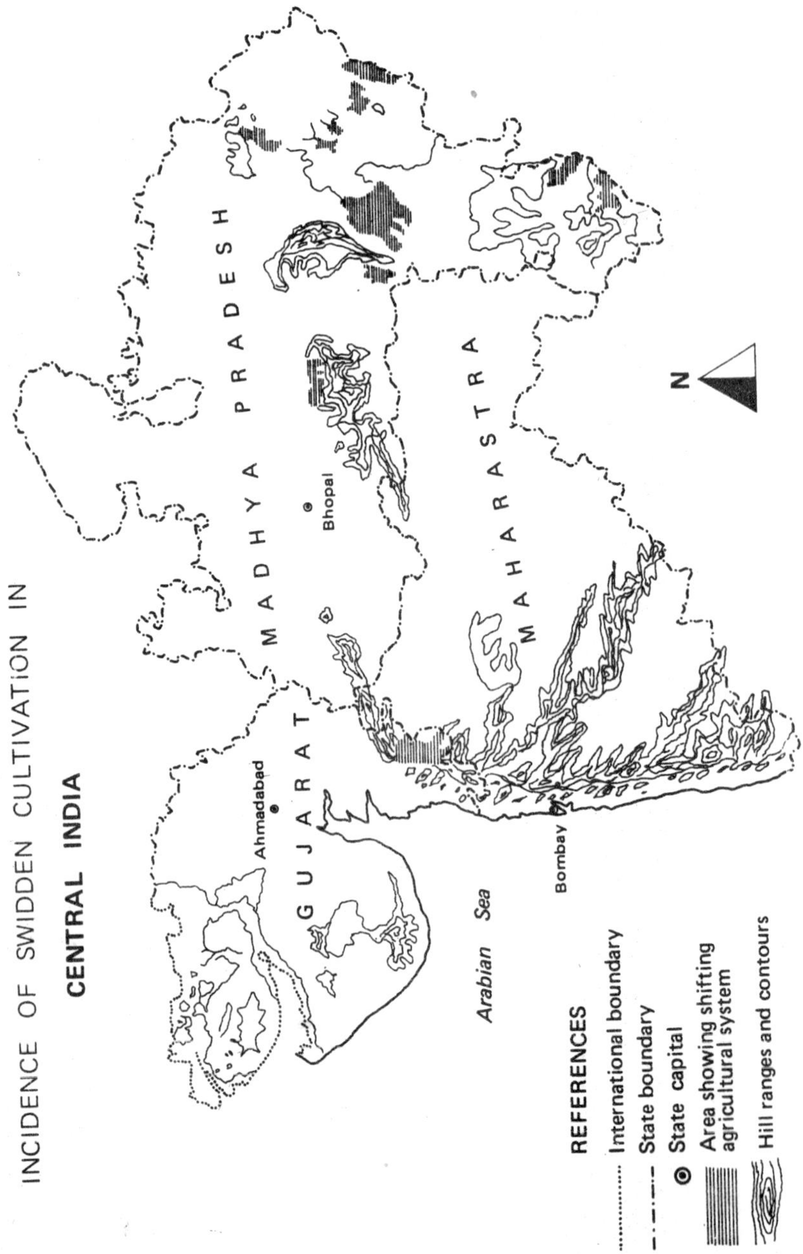
INCIDENCE OF SWIDDEN CULTIVATION IN
CENTRAL INDIA
MADHYA PRADESH
Bhopal
MAHARASTRA
GUJARAT
Ahmadabad
Arabian Sea
Bombay
N
REFERENCES
International boundary
State boundary
State capital
Area showing shifting agricultural system
Hill ranges and contours

INCIDENCE OF SWIDDEN CULTIVATION IN SOUTH INDIA

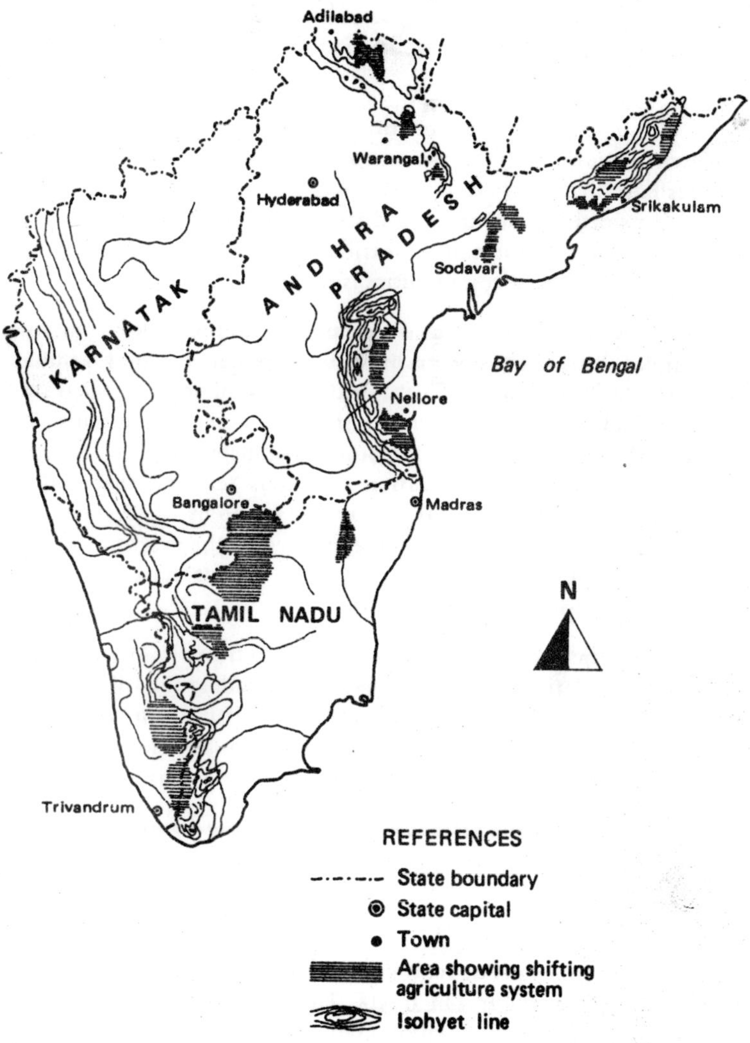

The Principal tribes inhabiting these regions and practising shifting cultivation are: Kurnbi, Bagata, Gadba, Kamar, Khond, Khond-Dhar, Konda-Kapur, Konda-Reddi, Koya, Mali, Manna Dhor, Nayak, Porya, Rena, Samanthu, and Savara of Andhra Pradesh; Bettakuruba, Jenukuruba, Kuman, Kunbi, Malakudia, Marati, and Soliga of Karnataka; Irular, Kader, Kurumba, Kurichiya, Mudnaggar and Paniyan of Kerala; and Kada, Kurumba, Malasar, Palayan, and Paniyan of Tamilnadu.

Though precise data on the extent of shifting cultivation in different regions of India are not available, a number of important studies have been carried out on the socio-economic life of the tribes practising shifting cultivation in different regions of India. However, the information on the nature of tribal economy and socio-economic structure of the tribal communities is rather scanty.

According to the Dhebar Commission Report (1962) the total area under shifting cultivation in India is estimated to be 1.4 million acres (560,000 hectares). To study the mode of shifting cultivation in India and its importance in the tribal economy in particular and Indian economy in general, the study conducted by D.C. Kaith in 1958 prior to the reorganization of States revealed that shifting cultivation constituted a vital part of the economy of 12 states. The following table presents the 1956 estimates of the extent of shifting cultivation practised by tribal people in various states and union territories of India.

It can be seen from the table that 109 tribes in 12 states comprising a population of about 2,644,200, excluding the tribal population of U.P. and Rajasthan, depended on shifting cultivation. Furthermore, nearly 439,918 acres were being annually cleared by these tribes. These figures reveal the vastness of the problems.

Following is the statewise break-up of the figures available in 1956.

Assam

In Assam, shifting cultivation locally known as *jumming* is mainly practised in the hill tracts. The tract, the approximate area cut annually, and the population involved are follows:

Table 3. The extent of shifting cultivation practised by the tribal people in various states and union territories of India (1956 estimates).*

Name of State	*No. of tribal communities practising shifting cultivation*	*No. of tribal households depending upon shifting cultivation*	*Total tribal population depending upon shifting cultivation*	*Total area of land utilized for shifting cultivation in acres*	*Kind of crops grown*
1.	*2*	*3*	*4*	*5*	*6*
Assam	9	194,000	970,000	512,000	Paddy, Cotton, Organges Chillies, Yarns, vegetables.
Orissa	20	200,000	1,000,000	400,000	Paddy, Pulses, turmeric, fruit trees.
Andhra Pradesh (A.P.)	10	40,000	200,000	96,000	–
Bihar	5	23,000	115,000	400	Paddy, Millets, Vegetables, Pulses.
Madhya Pradesh (M.P.)	15	600	30,000	44,000	Millets, Oil seeds and Pulses.
Bombay	10	5,000	25,000	723,000	Paddy, Millets and Oil seeds.
Mysore	5	2,800	14,000	2,500	Millets, Oilseeds, chillies.
Kerala	15	2,000	10,000	54,000	Paddy, Millets, Potato, Cotton, Oil seeds.
Madras	5	440	2,200	3,000	Hilly paddy, Millets, Maize Bean-opastures, fruit trees.
Uttar Pradesh (U.P.)	2	–	–	200	

Name of State	*No. of tribal communities practising shifting cultivation*	*No. of tribal households depending upon shifting cultivation*	*Total tribal population depending upon shifting cultivation*	*Total area of land utilized for shifting cultivation in acres*	*Kind of crops grown*
1.	*2*	*3*	*4*	*5*	*6*
Manipur	3	36,000	133,000	54,000	Millets, Potatoes, Paddy, Cotton, Oil-seeds.
Tripura	10	19,100	95,500	116,900	Paddy, Cotton, Jute Sugarcane Vegetable.
Others	Nil	Nil	Nil	Nil	
Total	109	528,940	2,644,200	1,355,300	

Source: D.C. Kaith, Shifting Cultivation practices in India, Indian Council of Agricultural research. Review series, New Delhi, 1956.

* For a breakdown of figures according to statistics, please see Kaith (1958).

Note: Some of these older tables use acres and sq. miles. In the text the following conversions are used: 1 acre = 0.4 hectares (ha); 1 sq. mile = 2.6 square kilometres (sq. km).

Table 4. Area cut annually in Assam*

Tract	*Approximate area cut annually (in sq. miles)*	*Total population*
Garo Hill distt.	125	190,000
United Mikir hill North-Kachar hill distt.	75	109,000
United Khasi and Jaintia hills distt.	200	300,000
Naga hill distt.	125	200,000
Mizo (Lushai hills) distt.	120	180,000
Plain dist. of Kamrup, Nowgong Cahar etc.	150	
Total	795	979,000

* The figures also include the territory and population now under the state of Meghalaya.

Tribes associated with this form of cultivation are Garo, Naga, Khasi, Mizo, Mikir etc.

Bihar

Swidden cultivation is normally done in the hilly tracts by tribes known as Kharia, in Singhbhum, Maler in Santhal Parganas.

Table 5. Area annually cut in Bihar and population involved

Tract	*Area*	*Population*
Singhbhum Distt.	40 acres	150
Santhal Pargana Distt.	400 acres	1,500
Total	440 acres	1,650

The soils in these areas are lateritic, shallow, and sandy loan in texture. The slope varies considerably from gentle to very steep. The annual rain fall is 55 inches (1,397 mm).

Bombay

Following is the extent of land and population involved in 1956 in Bombay State.

Table 6. Land and population in Bombay State*

District	*Total area brought under shifting cultivation annually in acres*	*Population living on shifting cultivation*
Kolaba	Abcut 8,000	13,000 to 15,000
Dangs	About 64,000	8,000 to 10,000
Belgaum	" 1,266	3,000
Kanara	" 783	10,000
Total	74,049	34,000 to 38,000

* This also includes population and territory now under Gujrat State.

In 1956, in Kolba district the tribes 'Thakur' and 'Katkar' carried out this form of shifting cultivation on areas selected on hill tops and slopes. The soil in this region is lateritic, shallow, and hard. The average rainfall varies between 100 to 105 inches (2,540 mm to 2,667 mm).

In Dang district, Kunbi, Konbani, Warli, Mavchi and Bhil are the principal tribes carrying on such cultivation. Most of the areas are rugged and hilly. The soil in the tract is red, grey, or black in colour. Rainfall is 60 to 80 inches (1,524 mm to 2,032 mm).

In Belgaum district, 'Kermbis' living in remote forest areas were practising shifting cultivation in about 10,000 acres of forest reserved by the Government for the purpose. The soil is poor and not suitable for permanent cultivation. The average rain fall is 130 inches (3,300 mm) and the areas are very steep.

Madras

In Coimbatore district the tribes Kadar, Malabar and Pulayan grow crops like ragi, thinai, samai, varage etc. after clearing the land and burning it; the same area is cultivated once in five years. In Ulandi, the areas are low lying, and the rainfall average is 70 inches

Table 7. Areas and population involved in shifting cultivation in 1956

Dist.	*Area in acres cut annually for shifting cultivation*	*Total population living on.*
Coimbatore Distt.		
(a) Anamalais	480	655
(b) Ulandi	50	50
Malabar Distt.		
(a) Ernad Taluk Private forest area	484	–
(b) Wallu Vanad		
Taluk Atta Pady Arrson	20,000 to 25,000	7,000 to 8,000
(c) Kozhikode, Kurumba and Kottayam, Wynaad and Chirakkal Taluk.	29,000	1,418
Nilgiri distt.		
Gudalu taluk	2,000 to 2,500	20,000 to 25,000
South Kanara dist		
Neria village	150	200
Total	42,528 to 48,028	29,323 to 33,322

(1,778 mm). In Anamalai, the areas are on gentle slopes. Soil is red or black. The average rainfall is about 100 inches (2,540 mm), minimum areas for the rehabilitation of these tribes in the above places is about four to five acres (1.6 ha to 2 ha).

In Kollegal divisions, 135 acres (54 ha) of land on free lease contract were being permanently cultivated by 59 families of Sholagars whom Kaith observed as both poor and backward and found them not interested in developing the land on their own. They do not practice shifting cultivation on these areas now but soil erosion was noted to be rampant and it was then suggested that it can be prevented by terracing the land at government expense.

In Malabar district as Kaith observed, the local people grow paddy in private forest areas in Ernad Taluk by clearing the forest. No definite rotation is followed.

Irular, Mudugar, Kurumba are the tribes associated with shifting cultivation in Attapady valley. Cultivation is done for 2 to 3 years. The area is later abandoned for 3 to 6 years.

Karichiyar, Paneyar, Irular, Malanaikan are the tribes carrying shifting cultivation in Kozikhode, Kottayam, Wynad, Kurumbranad, Chirakkal Taluks.

In Nilgiri district, the hill tribes, paniyar, Naiken, Kurumbar, were found to be practising shifting cultivation on slopes in Gudalur taluk, by growing hill paddy, ragi, sanrai, cholam, again hill paddy or vegetables in successive rotation, taking only one crop each year.

In south Kanara, the male Kudiya, carry what is known as 'Kumri cultivation' in the hilly areas of Neria, village. The same area is cultivated once in 2 to 3 years. The rainfall is very heavy. Suitable lands are not easily available.

Madhya Pradesh

The following is the 1956 estimate of the extent of land and population involved in shifting cultivation in Madhya Pradesh.

Table 8. Shifting cultivation in M.P.

Districts	*Area in acres cut annually.*	*Total population living on shifting cultivation*
Durg distt.	1,050	4,420
Bastar distt.	25,000 to 30,000	13,000
Chhindwara distt.	4,590	8,160
Chanda distt.	700	558
Balaghat distt.	2,994	1,217
Mandla distt.	120	230
Sarguja distt.	2,000	5,000
Raigarh distt.	340	680
Bilaspur distt.	2,772	6,930
Jashpur distt.	310	705
Total	39,876	40,890

In Bastar district the Maria, Muria and Gond cultivate only sloping areas of various degrees under what is locally known as the *Mashan* or *Penda* system.

In Chanda district the madia grow Khesari and Kodo on the same lines as above on the steep slopes with poor soil in hilly areas. The rain fall varies from 50 to 60 inches (1,270 mm to 1,524 mm).

In Balaghat district, the Baiga, and Gonds cultivate slopes having sandy loam soil crops such as *kodo, kutki madia, ramtilla, audi, kong sawa,* and *Makai.* The cultivation practices are similar to those adopted in the other districts.

In Mandla district, the Baiga carry on shifting cultivation by clearing the poor types of tal and mixed forest areas. Soil in the valley is of black cotton type, while on the flat hill tops mainly *murram* lies. The terrain is sloping to north and receives an annual rainfall or about 100 inches (2,540 mm).

In Raigarh district, the Panda, Kerwa and Majhwar grow crops such as *ashar, khedi, bedi, madia,* and *makai* (maize) cutting and burning the standing growth. Each family cultivated about two acres for 2 years and then abandoned the patch for 15 to 20 years. The soil is sandy loam and average rainfall is about 70 inches (1,778 mm).

In Sarguja district the Korwa, Kodaku, Agaria and Pande carry on cultivation locally known as *beera* on the same lives as in other district.

In Bilaspur district each family in Baigas raises the crop of *kodo kutki,* castor, mustard etc. over a piece of two acres of land for about 2 years and abandon the land thereafter.

In Jaipur district the Pahari Korwa, and Majhi carry on cultivation on hill slopes rich soil. The average rainfall in these areas is about 60 to 70 inches (1,524 mm to 1,778 mm).

Uttar Pradesh

Kaith in his study in 1956 found only two small pockets, one Lalitpur subdivision of the Jhansi district and the other in Rupin and Supin valleys in the upper reaches of the Tons valley in Tehri

Garhwal district where shifting cultivation was in vogue. No actual data about the populations involved in this area is available. In Jhansi district the Sahanya, a scheduled caste, carry on this type of cultivation with *Jowar* as main crop after clearing, felling and burning the slash and dibbling the seed before the monsoon without ploughing the land. The tract is flat and undulating of type of Vindhya highland having reddish sandy loam or clay loam soil. It has an annual rainfall of 40 to 50 inches (1,016 mm to 1,270 mm).

In Tehri Garhwal district the people practising shifting cultivation differ in customs, features etc. from the inhabitants of the rest of the Rawi Tehsil of the district. There are about 200 acres (80 ha) under shifting cultivation.

Manipur

The following figures give ample proof of the fact that shifting cultivation in Manipur was practised on a large scale in the 1950s.

Table 9. Shifting cultivation in Manipur

Total area of State hectares (ha)	*Area constituting valley proportion in hectares (ha)*	*Area constituting hills in in hectares (ha)*	*Area annually cut for shifting cultivation in hectares (ha)*	*Population involved.*
2,235,947	181,300	2,055,942	54,181	182,902

The tribes associated in this type of cultivation which is locally known as *Jhum* cultivation are Kuki Angami, Tangkhul Maring, Kabuie and Kachanaga. The pattern of shifting cultivation exists largely in the Manipur South and Manipur East districts.

Mysore (Karnataka)

In 1956 Kaith studied shifting cultivation as adopted by the hill tribes called the Betta Kuruba, Jenukuruba and soliga in the then Mysore state now Knoun as Karnataka.

Following is the distribution of Swiddening families in the State.

Table 10. Shifting cultivation practiced in the Area of Mysore (now called Karmataka)

Area	*Area under shifting cultivation. in hectares*	*Families concerned*
Hansur Range	14	18
Heggadadinakote Range	4	55
Kakanakote Range	28	40
Begur Range	10	15
Ainurmarigudi Range	12	12
Gundal Pet Range	8	8
Chamraj Nagar Range	8	10
Bandipur Range	4	8
Total	88	116

Orissa

Shifting cultivation is being carried out over large areas which are not suitable for permanent agriculture by tribes, the Bhuiya, Juang, Erengakol, and Konch, in hill tracts in north Orissa, north of the river Mahanadi and the areas in the district or Keonjhar, Sundergarh, Dhenkanal and Sambalpur. In south Orissa the Kondhs, Kutia, Kondh, Bunjia, Kamor Kond, Saora, Jalapa, Paroja, Gandba, Kojas, and others carry out shifting cultivation in the district of Ganjam, Koraput, Kalahandi. In between these two broad zones, there is a small patch in sonebra plateau in the extreme west of the state comprising of the tribes Binjhia and Kamar. Locally this type of cultivation is called *Rama* by Kond and *biringa* by Bhuinya in the north Orissa and *podu Gudia donge* and *Chas* in south. All these terms refer to the primitive types of cultivation carried out on the slopes exceeding 30°. However, terms like *dahi* in Sambalpur and *taila* in central and eastern Orissa are different from the podu cultivation; the former being practised on level ground, mild slopes or the hill. No exact data is available for this state. But yet from the available information given in the table below it is seen that a total area of about 13,000 square miles (33,800 sq km), involving a dozen tribes with a population of 1,100,000 was affected in 1956.

Table 11. Shifting cultivation in Orissa

District	*Area affected in sq. miles.*		*Population of connected tribe.*		*Total population involved.*
North Orissa					
Keonjhar		– 460	Bhuiya	– 20,000	28,000
			Juang	– 800	
Sundergarh	Bonae	– 300	Bhuiya	– 10,000	11,000
			Erengakol	– 1,000	
Dhenkanal	Pallahara	– 100	Bhuiya	– 2,600	2,600
Sambalpur	Barwa	– 360	Bhuiya	– 7,000	15,800
	Radhakol	– 150	Kondh	– 6,600	
			Kondh	– 2,200	
Total		1,270			57,400
South Orissa					
Kalahandi	Kalahandi	– 800	Kondh	– 111,000	119,300
	Kharian	– 200	Kutiya	– 1,300	
			Kondh	–	
			Kamor	– 1,600	
			Bhuiya	– 5,400	
Ganjam	Ganjam agency Kondhmals Baliguda and parlakhe-undi	– 4,500	Kondh Sarora	– 206,800	303,000
				– 35,600	
				– 600	
Koraput	Jeypore-Estate	– 5,000	Kondh	– 176,500	456,000
			Saora	– 52,500	
			Jatapu	– 15,200	
			Paroja	– 145,700	
			Godaba	– 34,300	
			Koya	– 28,000	
			Other	– 3,800	
	Total	10,500			878,300
Grand Total		11,770			935,700

Rajasthan

In this State Kaith (1957) studied the tribal people from hills and forests carrying the following two types of cultivation.

(1) *Dandakast* (in plain forest) and

(2) *Daikast* (In the hills).

These types are prevalent in the districts of Banswara, Dungarpur, in the Kerwas subdivision of Udaipur, Shahabad and Chhippabarod Tehsil in Kota district. No accurate data are available at hand, and whatever information on the extent of area under shifting cultivation could be gathered is given below:

Table 12. Area under cultivation in Rajasthan

District	*Area under cultivation*	
	in acres	*in hectares*
Banswara distt.	100	40
Dungarpur distt.	100	40
Udaipur distt.	200	80
Shahabad tehsil	21,300	8,520
Chhippabarod tehsil	100	40
Total	21,800	8,720

The tribes, Bhil, Sahria, Meena, Bagri, Grasia including Jogi, and Dholi, of Banswara, and Dungarpur cultivate on moderate to steep hill slopes having poor soil and rainfall varying between 30 to 40 inches (762 mm to 1,016 mm).

Tripura

Tripura is a hilly territory and is entirely made up of parallel ranges or hills extending north to south and alternated with narrow valleys. The total area of the state is 41,116 square miles out of which 66 per cent is covered with forests. Around 47,000 hectares are under swidden involving a total population of 95,501 distributed in ten major tribes.

Swidden Cultivation in India in the 1960s

A further study by Roy Burman and P.S. Sharma (1970) provides us a detailed study of the different tribes practising shifting cultivation in different regions of India in the 1960s. The table on pages 30-32 makes a regionwise comparative study of tribes practising shifting cultivation in the 1960s.

Shifting Cultivation in the 1970s

It is not possible to make a comparative estimate of the area and population involved in shifting cultivation in the 1950s and 1970s due to inadequate data. The figures on shifting cultivation in Northeast India in 1976 are, however, available.

From the data available earlier and that of Table 14 on page 33 it has been found that about 2.5 million people of Northeast India eke out a living from Jhum cultivation involving 2.7 million hectares of land.

Table 13. Tribes practising shifting cultivation in various states and union territories, population involved in swidden and the area covered under shifting cultivation 1961 estimates

Sl. No.	Name of the State/Union Territory	Tribes practising shifting cultivation	Population depending on shifting cultivation (Approx) 1961	Area covered under shifting cultivation (in acres) 1961	Districts and divisions where shifting cultivation is carried on.
1.	2	3	4	5	6
1.	Assam	Abor, Chakma, Dimasa, Garo, Jaintia, Karbi, Khasi, Lushai, Lalung, Mikir, Mizo, Naga.	200,000	96,000	Karbi Anglong, North Cachar Hills.
2.	*Arunachal Pradesh	Hill Miri, Dafta, Padam, Gallong, Neshi, Sulung, Tagin, Na, Mara, Wancho, Nocte, Tangsa, Gangri, Aka, Monpa, Singpho.	–	–	Kameng, Lohit, Subanisiri, Tirap and Siang.
3.	*Meghalaya	Khasi, Garo, Jaintia, War, Pnar.	–	–	Garo Hills, Jaintia Hills.
4.	Nagaland	Sema, Ao, Lohta, Konyan, Rengma, Tangkhul, Naga etc.	–	–	Tuengsang
5.	*Mizoram	Lushai, – –	–	–	Lushai Hills
6.	Manipur	Angami, Hmar, Kabui, Kachanaga, Kuki, Mao, Maring, Tangkhul	183,000	54,000	Manipur East, Manipur South.
7.	Tripur	Chakma, Garo, Halam, Jhumia, Jamatia, Kuki, Lushai, Mag, Noatia, Reang, Tripuri	95,500	116,900	Sadar, Khowai, Kailashahar, Kamalpur, Dharmanagar, Udaipur, Sonemura, Belonia and Amarpur Subdivision.

Sl. No.	Name of the State/Union Territory	Tribes practising shifting cultivation	Population depending on shifting cultivation (Approx) 1961	Area covered under shifting cultivation (in acres) 1961	Districts and divisions where shifting cultivation is carried on.
1.	2	3	4	5	6
8.	West Bengal	Toto	N.A.	N.A.	Jalpaiguri.
9.	Orissa	Bhwiyan or Bhuyan, Binjhia, Bonda, Didayi, Erenga Kol, Gadaba, Jatapu, Juang, Kamar, Kondh, Koya, Kutia Kondh, Pengo, Paraja, Saora	935,700	400,000	Keonjhar, Sundergarh, Dhankanal, Sambalpur, Kolahandi, Ganjarn and Koraput districts and Phulbani, Baliguda, Jeypore and Nalanangiri Subdivisions.
10.	Bihar	Birjhia, Kharia, Maler, Norwe, Mal Paharia, Sauria, Paharia	115,000	436	Singhbhum, Santhal Parganas, Ranchi.
11.	Madhya Pradesh	Agriya, Baiga, Bharia, Gond, Kamar, Konku, Kondaku, Korwa, Manjhi, Madia/Maria, Majhwar, Mawasi, Pande.	30,000	947,680**	Durg, Bastar, Bilaspur, Chhindawara, Balaghat Raigarh and Surguja.
12.	Rajasthan	Bhil, Sahria, Meena, Bagri, Gradia, Jogi, Dholi	N.A.	N.A.	N.A.
13.	**Gujrat	Bhil, Konka, Kunbi, Kokanis, Mavehi, Varli	25,000**	72,300**	The Dangs and Some parts of Surat.
14.	**Maharashtra	Bhil, Halkki, Katkari, Kunbi, Kumari-Marahta, Konakari, Mavebi, Maria-Gond, Thakur, Wakkal, Warli			Kolaba, South-Chand division and Janjira subdivision.
15.	Karnataka	Bettakuruba, Jenururuba, Kumbi, Kunbia, Kumar, Malekudia, Marati, Soliga.	14,000	2,500	Interior mountanious tracts of Belgaum of South-Kanara district.

Sl. No.	Name of the State/Union Territory	Tribes practising shifting cultivation	Population depending on shifting cultivation (Approx) 1961	Area covered under shifting cultivation (in acres) 1961	Districts and divisions where shifting cultivation is carried on.
1.	2	3	4	5	6
16.	Andhra Pradesh	Begata, Gadaba, Hill Reddi, Kammar, Khond, Kolam, Kotiyar, Koyas, Kenda-Kanpur, Konda Reddi, Rond-Dhor, Mali, Manna Dhor, Nayak, Porya, Rena, Samantha, Savara.	200,000	96,000	Adilabad, Srikakulam district Agency tracts, visakhapatnam East Godavari, West Godavari and Warangal.
17.	Tamil Nadu	Irula, Kadar, Kurumbar, Madigar, Malanaikan, Malasar, Malekudiyar, Naickers, Pulayar, Paniyan, Sholagar	2,200	3,000	Coimbatore and Nilgiris.
18.	Kerala	Irula, Kurumba, Kurichiyar, Malanaikan, Muduga, Paniyar	10,000	54,000	Attapaddy Amson, Malabar district and Vaunvanad Talug.

* In 1956 and 1961 Arunachal Pradesh, Meghalaya, Nagaland and Mizoram were the parts of Assam and Gujrat and Maharastra were the parts of Bombay state.

** Roy Burman and Sharma in their work show the extent of land in 1956 as 947,680 acres whereas Mahapatra puts it as 44,000 acres only. However, to our analysis the figure presented by Mahapatra appears to be more accurate.

Sources: ii) B.K. Roy Burman and P.S. Sharma, "Tribal Agriculture in India", Indian Journal of Agricultural Economics, Vol. 25, No. 3, 1970, pp. 159-166.

iii) Jayanta, Sarkar, "An observation on some economic aspects of the tribes of Arunachal Pradesh" (paper presented in the "workshop on Tribal Economy" organized by Anthropological Survey of India, Calcutta) February, 1977.

Table 14. Area under, and population dependent on, shifting cultivation in north-east India 1976*

State/Union territory	*Area under Jhum thousand hectares)*	*Area Jhumed Annually (thousand hectares)*	*No. of Families*	*Jhummed per family (hectares)*
Arunachal Pradesh	248.58	92.00	148	0.62
Assam				
a. Mikir hills	415.10	54.00	45	1.20
b. N.C. Hills	83.20	15.60	13	1.20
Manipur	100.00	60.00	50	1.20
Meghalaya	416.00	76.00	68	1.12
Mizoram	604.03	61.61	45	1.37
Nagaland	608.00	73.54	80	0.92
Tripura	220.79	22.30	43	0.51
Total	2,695.70	455.05	492	0.92

* *Sources:* 1) Director of Evaluation and monitoring, N.E. Council, Shillong.

2) R.K. Mukherjee, "Some Social Constraints to Agricultural Development in North East India" North-Eastern Affairs, Annual Issue, 1975.

Chapter Three

SWIDDEN ECONOMY AND OPERATIONS

Out of the total area considered to be under Swidden cultivation only a small extent of land is brought under cultivation in a particular year. This proportion of land depends on the number of years a plot is cultivated consequently and thereafter is allowed to lie fallow before cultivation is resumed. For instance, if a plot of land is cultivated consecutively for two years and then is allowed to lie fallow for eight years, then one quarter of the land available for shifting cultivation would be actually under cultivation in a particular year. However, the area to be cultivated in a particular year and the rotation cycle are also influenced by a number of other factors such as the fertility of the soil of the area undertaken and availability of manpower and so on. From our study this fact also comes to light that fallowing is not a consciously planned attempt to restore the fertility of the soil but is forced by the hard natural conditions which lead to the depletion of the fertility of the soil (Dar, 1970).

Land ownership

In most of the hill areas of Northeast India, land is owned by the community as a whole. Individual ownership of land is recognised in certain areas usually confined to homestead and settled farm land. Each village operates in a particular demarcated area and the power of distribution of land for cultivation to individual families is vested in the headman or the village council (Saikia, 1976). The headman or the village council selects a fertile forested area within the demarcated area at the beginning of the agricultural year and distributes land to each individual family of the village according to necessity. But besides necessity, the size of land allocated to a family depends to a large extent on the number of working hands of the family.

Usually the households cultivate plots selected through various means, including divination. Ordinarily, a plot remains under cultivation for one or two years, after that it is abandoned and the household concerned cleans up another patch of land for cultivation. After a lapse of a number of years, varying from five or six to 12 to 15 or at times even more, they may return to the same plot. It is not always that the same household cultivates the same plot of land. Very frequently individual households do not have absolute ownership over the land cultivated by them; their rights are of the nature of usufruct. They can hold the land so long as they make effective use of it. As soon as they stop their operation, their rights cease. In the next cycle any other person belonging to the same community may take up the plot. If, however, a person plants a tree on a plot of land, his right over the tree continues in many communities. As a result, a curious situation sometimes comes into existence, where the agricultural produce on a plot of land belongs to one person, but the trees on the same plot, belong to another (Burman, 1960).

It has been found that due to non-fixity of tenurial rights, the farmers naturally have very little attachment to the land they operate. They do not take interest in the improvement of the land for future use. A tendency to improve land is noticed in areas where land is privately owned.

Among the Karbi of Assam and among other tribes of Arunachal Pradesh where land is communally owned, one can cultivate a plot of land according to ones choice. The village headman enjoys the power to settle disputes relating to sharing of jhum land among the villagers. Inter-village disputes regarding jhum land is very rare as the villages are scattered widely over the hills the distance between one village and another being usually not less than 5 miles (8 km). When there is dispute between the households regarding jhum land the dissatisfied group may leave the village and set up a new village with a headman of their own (Saikia, 1968).

Among the Adis of Lushai hills the village forms the largest agricultural unit, each having its own jhuming fields within its territorial boundaries, marked by such natural features as hills or streams. The demarcation of the boundaries takes place through various processes. Similar is the pattern of landownership among the Idus of the Diban Valley in Arunachal Pradesh.

In Manipur a chief setting up a new village used to pay some sort of tribute to the chief of the community within whose jurisdiction the territory acquired by him was considered to lie. Sometimes physical might was the determining factor in settling the question of right. In many areas of Northeast India feuds relating to village boundaries were quite frequent; and even now they are not uncommon. In many areas within the boundary of the village, there is clanwise demarcation of land.

The Khasi hills district of Meghalaya is divided into Rajs ruled by Siems (Raja), Lyngdoh (priest), Pator, Basan and Sardar who are administrators of each Raj. Each member of the Raj is entitled to cultivate any vacant land as much as he pleases. As long as he cultivates, the land belongs to him. If a man does not cultivate land under his occupation for three consecutive years, it reverts to the Raj and some other person can cultivate it. (Gohain and Saikia, 1979).

Among the Garo, the machong or lineage group is the owner of a particular akhing (community land) where members of that machong have the right to carry on shifting cultivation. In Garo hills of Meghalaya the hill mouzas are divided into several Akings, each under a Aking Nokma (headman) who technically owns land on behalf of his clansmen. The Aking Nokma has the power to distribute land among his clansmen for the purpose of jhuming. (Saha and Barkotky, 1969).

Among the Chero of Manipur, the land of the village under shifting cultivation is in the possession of the village community as a whole. The chief does not have any extraordinary right over the land. All members of the village community have equal right to any part of that village. No areas are marked out as areas of clans and families.

Among the Hmar of United Mikir and Cachar Hills of Assam there is no family-wide demarcation of land. Among most of the Kuki and Mizo group of tribes, the chief is the sole proprietor of the land and the villagers have to take land on a rental basis. On the other hand, among the Mikirs, it has been noted that once a plot of land has been cultivated by a particular household, the same household will cultivate that very plot of land after being left fallow for a certain period.

Among the Tangkhul Naga of Manipur East district land disputes arise from time to time particularly among the plot owners since there is no record showing the area of ownership maintained by the Revenue Department. At the same time the interval between each cultivation of the block of land is too long to remember the exact boundary and the interested individual owner changes the stone boundary extending his plot of land (Hungyo, 1977).

Among the Angami of Manipur a greater part of jhum land is individual property and subject to life interests and mortgages, which may be sold or otherwise disposed of at the will of the owner, though when selling an ancestral field the vendor retains a small fragment in nominal ownership lest he die or suffer misfortune. In several Angami villages a certain amont of jhum land which is reserved for thatching grass or for the preservation of cane for bridges, is the common property of a kindred or a clan or of the whole village. The cultivation of land of this sort is settled either by a system of general consent or by a system of 'grab' provided it does not exceed the limit and deprive others of their share. Usually the ownership of the first claimant is recognised for two years. A series of cultivations by the same man in the same place appears to set up a private right to the particular plot, and there is no doubt that in this way private rights in land have arisen. In some transfrontier villages all land is still common property of the village. Jhum land that has not yet become the subject of private rights can not of course be sold except by the clan or kindred owning it, though with their consent it might be possible for a man to sell his share in the common rights. Jhuming, however, is of quite secondary importance in Angami country except for the chakma village. For this reason common rights in land still survive. Where jhuming is the normal form of cultivation, private rights have superseded common rights, as among the Semas and Aos (Hutton, 1969).

According to Gohain (1953) some villages possess certain common land called *molipatat* ownership, the right of which rests with the whole village. Where there is a shortage of land, cultivation may be carried out on this land by the needy people of the village with the consent of the village council. Besides this, all arable lands are divided into two categories: *patat*, or rotation zone for jhuming by the villagers; and *arik* or field plot of individual households within each *patat*. The boundaries of *ariks* are marked with heaps of stones placed at regular intervals to make the right of a permanent nature. The rights of cultivators over such lands, are passed over to the male descendants. In case a family is short of land a special meeting of the village tries to find a clan with surplus land and if there is any, they get if leased out temporarily to the needy family while the original right of such land rests with the lender class. Such a temporary arrangement is usually for two years.

The *patat* ownership pattern is found to be prevalent among the Padam and Gallong of Arunachal Pradesh and Abor of Assam. The agricultural land throughout Subansiri, Kamla, Lower Kemang and Papu valleys is practically owned by individuals within overall control of the village. Each village has its own area ranging from one hill to another. An individual who wants to open jhum land can do so on his own. A similar system is found in the Tangsa villages of that region (Sarkar, 1977). Among the Sherdukpen of Arunachal there exists a system of limited individual ownership in respect of jhum land. Once an individual brings a jhum plot under cultivation, he has the prerogative of cultivating the same plot, on completion of the jhum cycle after a number of years, but he cannot sell the jhum plot under any circumstances. He can, however allow others to cultivate the plot, if for any reason he cannot do it, in a particular jhum cycle. The various clans in the village have their own clan land. Such land includes distant forest areas and steep rocky forest where honey can be found (Roy Burman, 1971:66). Among the Singhho of Arunachal, the chief is the master of all land within his territory but in fact individual rights to land are recognised and respected. No transaction of land, however, can take place without the chief's knowledge and permission. A similar system of land ownership is prevalent among the Khamti, Wanchoo and Nocte of Arunachal Pradesh (Sarkar, 1977).

In Sema and Kanyak regions of Nagaland the land ownership right is vested in the village chief and it passes by inheritance on the basis of blood relationship. But even in these regions, the actual cultivator of the land has a perpetual right of cultivation and that right is handed down by inheritance. In Nagaland the problem of fragmentation of land has not arisen to any large extent, excepting among the Angami.The Angami and Chakesang of Nagaland have individual ownership system of land. Every individual owns land and enjoys every right over it. The right is permanent, heritable and transferable; ownership of land being either by inheritance or by purchase. However, there are many cases where land and forest are held jointly by Khel (clan or lineage), but this system is on the wane (Das, 1977).

Among the Ao Naga the individuals, who are in need of land, take the same on lease from individuals having surplus land. In such case also, the land is reverted to the original owner after two years.

Among the Maria and other tribes of the Abujhmar Hills of Bastar (M.P.) disputes over distribution of land among families are practically unknown, mainly because of the fact that there is ample land for all. In the Lushai Hills also there is no shortage of land. The land is distributed in a more democratic way through lottery where everyone has an equal chance. As they are educated and far less primitive in comparision with the Hill Marias, they are able to evolve such a system. Among the Juang, a similar primitive tribe of the Keonjhar Hills, Orissa, disputes over distribution of land is common as there is shortage of land and pressure of population (Bose, 1967).

Among the Pauri Bhuiya or Hill Bhuiya of Western Keonjhar and Eastern Bonai the land coming under Swidden cultivation are generally of two types; First, the swidden land free to all villagers and held by the tenure of 'corporate village ownership' as village common land and forests, second the flat upland or 'gura' land for swidden cultivation held by the family. (Mahapatra, 1965).

Among the Baiga of Madhya Pradesh there is no clan or tribal leadership. The measurement and division of plots among the families is done by Forest Department officials. The land is owned by the family. (Nag, 1958).

Among the Koya of Andhra Pradesh cultivation bestows possession. The man who is acknowledged as the cultivator of a field is also the owner of it. However, cultivation does not confer rights of permanent possession. If a cultivator allows his fields to lie fallow for three years, he relinquishes all rights in them. Prior cultivation does not establish residual rights for when a field has lain fallow for three years, any Koya cultivator has a right to clear and crop it (Tyler, 1974).

Jhum cycle

The typology of swidden along with the cycle, consecutive cultivation period and the subsequent fallowing period which is known as jhum cycle, differs from tribe to tribe. The fallowing period is mainly dependent upon the density of population of a particular area, availability of suitable hill slope, composition of soil and capacity of the same to recoup its fertility through natural process (as the tribals traditionally do not put any other fertilizer to augment the productivity).

The higher the density of population the shorter the jhum cycle. The following tables shows the variance in jhum cycle in different regions of tribal India:

Table 15. Variance in jhum cycle in regions of tribal India

Tribe and the region	*Period of cultivation in years*	*Fallow period in years*
Khasi (Meghalaya)	1	4 to 5
Garo (Meghalaya)	2	7
Mikir (Assam)	1 to 2	5
Sema Naga (Assam)	2	10 to 12
Lakher (Assam)	1	8 to 10
Dimasa (Assam)	1 to 2	10 to 12
Lushai (Assam, Tripura and Mizoram)	2	2 to 3 (Bambooing 7 to 8 (Dense forest)
Lhota Naga	2	8 to 10
Rengma Naga	1 to 2	20 to 30
Ao Naga	2	10
Angami Naga (Manipur)	2	5 to 15
Mao (Manipur)	1	10
Kabui, Maring and Chero (Manipur)	1 to 2	10
Hmar	1	6
Adis (NEFA)	2 to 3	10 to 20
Jhumia (Tripura)	1	about 10
Reang (Tripura)	1	7 to 9
Koya (Orissa)	3	10
Orissa (Keonjhar hills)	2	12
Maler (Chotanagpur)	1	5

The review of swidden cultivation prevailing among the tribes of India brings to light the fact that over the past few decades the jhuming cycle has been abridged from a longer margin to a shorter one. For instance in the case of Nagaland it has been reduced to 6-10 years while it was 12-15 years a few decades ago.

The main factors influencing the jhum cycle are a) increase in population, and b) destruction of forests.

Shifting of residence

In the tribal regions where residences are not shifted the distance of agricultural land from the residence is an important consideration. In Northeast India generally the tribal communities practise shifting cultivation. There are however, some tribal communities which frequently change their residence because of various factors including the impermanence of their cultivation. The names of the Mikirs and the Kuki group of tribes could be mentioned under this category. Among the Marias of Abujhmar hills the villages also shift along with the shifting of *penda* fields (Bose, 1967). A hill Mikir village or a karbi village in karbi Anglong district of Assam cannot be considered a geographical unit because of the frequent change of site of the village. As they shift to new localities at almost regular intervals the construction of permanent houses at a particular site is considered useless. In general, however, the villages are usually fixed in one locality but their jhum fields shift to a new place along with the jhum cycle. Moreover, the size of a village is usually small. In some cases only four or five households, situated 2 or 3 miles (3 to 5 km) apart constitute one village. It is rather difficult to take up agricultural development plans in such small, isolated, migratory and semi-nomadic villages.

Among the Jhumias of Tripura the shifting of villages was common in the past. Now it is very rare. In some cases among the Jhumias some individual families shift when a man of one village, who finds it difficult to co-operate with the rest of the villagers, joins another where he has some relations or sees better prospects for jhuming.

The Tangas of Tirap district in Arunachal Pradesh establish field-homes near the land where almost all the family members stay during agricultural activities.

The shifting cultivators of Tripura may be classified in the following three categories:

(i) Jhumias by choice:– In this category are such tribal people who have got permanent land and a homestead, but, being closer to the hills, jhum a small area only to produce cotton and some vegetables which are easily grown in the jhum. The tribes coming under this category are – Jamatia, Noatia and a few Holams and Riangs, who with the patronage of the king, got some special privileges and encouragement in acquiring land. A large number of Chakmas and Mugs, who came to Tripura only in the recent past, occupied lands either by reclamation or by driving out others from a particular area and started ploughing. (ii) Incipient Sedementary Farmers:– This category consists of those tribal people who have reclaimed some land in the foot hills and loongas and have started plough cultivation out of their own choice. But because of inadequate income, owing either to insufficient land tilled or insufficient plough farming, they practice jhuming as a supplementary source of income. (iii) Pure Jhumias:– Pure Jhumias entirely depend on jhuming for production of their food and do not possess plain land for plough cultivation. They are not conversant with the methods of ploughing at all.

Intensity of labour among shifting cultivators

Unlike permanent or terrace cultivation shifting cultivation is labour-intensive and is usually carried out through numerous forms of co-operative labour outside the family. In the shifting cultivation human labour and land are the principal factors of production.

In most of the tribal societies, one is not accustomed to work as an agricultural labourer. Hence one is very much dependent on family labour which is the vital input under shifting cultivation. It is precisely because of this factor that the size of swidden depends mainly on the number of able-bodied members in a swidden cultivator family. Marriage is an important source of procuring more working hands. Among the Jhumia the institution of marriage requiring the prospective groom to stay in his father-in-law's house for a period of three to five years provides an important source of labour supply. This practice among them is known as 'Jamai-Khatka'. During the period of Jamai-Khatka the prospective groom has to engage in all work connected with Jhumming.

In a study of the Dafla in Assam (Saikia, 1968) it is observed that there is an abundance of jhum land and thus the cultivators having more working hands at their disposal can produce more crops. As it is observed; there is usually no provision of agricultural labour among the shifting cultivators, the economically well off cultivators either purchase slaves or procure wives to work for them. In such an economic network polygyny is a natural tendency. Procuring more than one wife is considered as a sound investment of surplus wealth to bring more working hands to the family. Since slavery is now illegal, marriage is the only way for the tribe to get additional working hands for a family. The system of polygyny appears to be common among many other tribes where it is used as a means to procure more labour. A change in the shifting cultivation system would also obviously lead to a change in the social priorities and in the system of living among these tribes.

Following, are the normal labour requirements for different agricultural operations in Kanther Terang village in Karbi Anglond district of Assam*

Table 16. Labour requirements Kanther Terang village

a)	Felling trees, cutting over growth and clearing jungle	27 man days per acre
b)	Tillage and sowing	12 " " " "
c)	Weeding	9 " " " "
d)	Harvesting	15 " " " "
	Total	63 " " " "

* *Source:* P.D. Saikia, Changes in Mikir Society, Agro-Economic Research Centre for N.A. India, Jorhat, 1968.

Table 17. Average Number of Mand days (8 hours a day)*

	Male	*Female*
1. Housing building	20	–
2. Watch house construction	10	–
3. Making of tools and Implements	10	–
4. Field work in Jhum	150	100
5. Domestic work	30	150
6. Collection, fishing, hunting	30	50
Total	250	300

* P.K. Mahapatra, 'Handbook on Koya: Economic activities and quest for food' Adibasi, Vol. XI, No. 4, 1969-70, p. 23.

Among the shifting cultivators of Agalgri area of Meghalaya the following are the normal labour requirements:

There is gross division of labour among the Jhumias. Men play the leading role in jhum cutting operations and clearance of fields, requiring greater physical strength. Women take up less strenuous jobs like sowing, watching and harvesting which spread over the longer part of the year. The data available from Northeast India show that Jhumia remain unemployed for 100 days a year for lack of jobs. These man days are lost due to absence of any initiative either by themselves or the administration of that region to implement any scheme which could utilize this surplus manpower by engaging them in terracing, land reclamation, afforestation, horticulture, road building on some basic agro-industries.

In Meghalaya there is no agricultural labour class among other tribes excepting the Khasis and the Jayantias. Every able-bodied person can work on communal land for himself and hence hardly anybody offers labour for hire.

Compared to paddy cultivation in the plains the Apatani paddy cultivation (under jhum) in Arunachal Pradesh is far more labour intensive. The preliminary tillage operation is done during the winter before the onset of heavy rains, with iron hoes, and puddling the soil is done with the feet. This takes a lot of their time and the activities involve extensive labour (Saikia and Kalita, 1979, 82). In the narrow and broad villages in Arunachal Pradesh the landowner seeks the help of kin for preparation of the jhum field. The cutting, clearing and burning of jhum is generally done by the men and the work of sowing, weeding, harvesting and bringing the crops from the field to the granary is done by the females. In the Padam village of Arunachal the male population is divided into four main groups based on age and marital status. These groups co-operate with each other according to the need. In exchange for their services the groups get a share of the produce which is used in feasting or for similar purposes.

The Tangsa also seek the help of their villagers. Those who render their services are served with meals and rice beer (*chol*) thrice a day. The Bagni of Papu valley too adopt similar methods of recruiting a labour force. One member from each family renders his services in clearing the jhum field (haram) of the wanchi chief.

Shifting cultivation among the Koya too is found to be labour intensive. In a field study conducted in the late 1960s it was found that for clearing a plot of about two acres (0.8 ha) of land it took about 42 man days (P.K. Mahapatra, 1969-70 : 23).

Among the Maler every family has to participate in clearing the field, hence the family running short of working hands engages Santhal and the Mal Pahariya of the neighbouring villages as labourers. Sometimes the Santhals also clear the forest on contract and get half the felled trees of the Kurwa on a fixed date. The owners of the plot also join the labourers in the agricultural operation known as *dari nide*.

For the Koyas of Andhra Pradesh clearing the forest for new podu is also hard work. Including previously cleared fields the total area cultivated by a man is estimated at four acres (1.6 ha) per year. The size of the podu field virtually depends upon the number of able bodied workers in a family or co-operating kindred or lineage segment. In podu cultivation the close agnatic relatives co-operate by locating their fields adjacent to one another and cutting and burning them at the same time.

A review of the pattern of shifting cultivation shows that among a large number of shifting cultivator tribes it is labour intensive and its success depends largely on the availability of a labour force. Since hired labour is seldom available, shifting cultivation must depend on a co-operative labour force.

Supplementary sources of subsistence

We also find many of the shifting cultivator tribes adopting supplementary sources of subsistence. When the jhum produce is not adequate, it is supplemented by hunting, fishing, and the collection of vegetables, roots and tubers from the forests. All these practices are not conducive to the maximum utilization of family labour on individual farms.

The Maler sell a larger part of the wood in the weekly market to buy food grain at the beginning of the agricultural season because at that time they have hardly any grain left. The economy of the Maler family is further supplemented by hunting and gathering. For the Kamars of M.P. however, hunting is not at all a regular source of food supply because of forest game rules and watch kept by the court of ward officials. They do a bit of hunting by stealth. Nevertheless, the Kamar use fishing as an important source of food next to shifting cultivation. Hunting and fishing are the important sources of livelihood for the tribes of Lushai Hills and the Hill Maria of Bastar region. Certain edible plants are also consumed by the people to save themselves from hunger in times of crop failure. Hunting is more popular in the foot hills than in the interior.

Economic structure

Mostly the economy of the shifting cultivators has been found to be of limited and self sufficient nature. However, their economy has been conspicuously influenced by the social milieu. Usually there is little marketable surplus with the shifting cultivators. Their marketing facilities are limited and the extent of monetization is restricted. The surplus produce is exchanged with traditional goods such as brass bells, beads and in some cases salt, utensils, dry fish and clothes.

The Juang area is deficient in food. Storing of crops is not as common as in the Lushai Hills or in the Abujhmar Hills. For purchasing the items of basic necessities such as clothing, utensils, implements and food items, they trade their cash crops such as russi or oilseed. For the Idu Mishmi the forest within the village boundaries provides the villagers with nearly all their needs; bamboo and thatch for building houses, firewood, cane for making mats, baskets and other household articles.

Among the Jhumia, jhuming represents a uniquely self sufficient economy. The self-sufficiency has of course been broken down to a considerable extent by the impact of their contact with the plainsmen. However, the essential characteristics of a subsistence economy still persists. In the past the Jhumias produced everything they consumed. They did not produce for exchange but only for consumption. However, among their crops, cotton and sesamum were commercially important. These commercial crops brought them in contact with businessmen who induced them to produce a surplus of cotton and sesamum to exchange for salt, tools, metal-ware and other necessary items. Subsequently, money entered their life as a medium of exchange. The introduction of money in the economic life of the Jhumias brought a vital change in their socio-economic relationship.

Nevertheless, the economic change brought about by the introduction of money has not completely eliminated the basic feature of the self-sufficient Jhumia economy. They come to the market to buy a number of items such as salt, Shidal (fermented fish), tobacco, leaves and molasses for preparing such items as tobacco, cooking oil and cloths, but none of these is absolutely necessary to be purchased from the market. They have either the indigenous method of producing them or have substitutes for them.

In the whole operation of jhuming the most critical period for Jhumia is from *Ashar* (mid-Jume) to *Bhadra* (mid-August). Generally at this time most of the jhumia families run short of food. But this is the period for weeding and watching the jhum and without these tasks being done jhum will not be successful. In such hours of crisis the Jhumias take credit from the mahajans (money-lenders) in the form of a crop advance called dadam. Usually the rate of interest is 50 per cent or above. The system of dadam virtually wrecks the Jhumia economy. Once trapped in the vicious circle of money lender the Jhumia shifting cultivators seldom escape. After paying back the dadam the Jhumia has hardly enough food-stock sufficient to support him up to the end of the agricultural year and thus a poor Jhumia has to come back to the money lender at the close of the jhum yera. The dadam becomes a recurring feature in the life of poor Jhumias.

In the beginning, when jhuming was dependent on free co-operative labour the yield was more or less equal. But due to some factors external to the system such as destruction of crops by pests and wild animals, or owing to someon's illness at the time of jhum work, some jhumias might get an inadequate yield. Then they would borrow money to help their family subsist and for procuring seeds at the time of jhuming in the following year. The leaders take the re-payment in the form of labour through which they manage to do jhuming on a bigger plot. Here comes a disparity between the two types of Jhumias. Inequality of income and economic status that is observed among the Jhumias today owes its origin to such a sequence of events.

Selection of jhum plot

In the selection of a plot for shifting cultivation a number of factors are taken into consideration. The following types of land are preferred for shifting cultivation among the Ao Nagas:

1. Land which was left fallow in the last cycle of cultivation in the block, i.e., land lying fallow for twenty years or more;

2. Land which has more sun and where fewer weeds grow;

3. Land facing east, as in such land fewer weeds grow and paddy thrives better; and

4. Level land where soil does not erode.

Before starting felling operations the Kamar select suitable levelled patches of land lying in between two slopes having a regular supply of water. The Lushai prefer bamboo forests for shifting cultivation. Jhumias of Tripura always prefer a bamboo forest to any other type for the jhum plots. The Jhumias also have to avoid elephant tracks in selection of the Jhum plots. They prefer a hill, one side of which is steep while the other three sides are with slanting slopes and are sorrounded by marshy lands. Under such surroundings a jhum is free from plunder by elephants. The availability of a water resource is also a major consideration in selecting the plot of land as the Jhumias have to stay at the jhum site for a considerable period. A plot close to a brook is much preferred.

In selecting the plot for Kurwa cultivation the Maler of Rajmahal Hill seriously consider whether the fertility of the field has adequately recuperated. This is indicated by the level of vegetation there. They do not select the Khallu Kurwa field very far from the village. Otherwise, it would be difficult to protect the crops from wild animals and thieves. They also do not use the plot near burial grounds and sacred groves because they think that the dead ancestors, evil spirits and Gosain (God) will get angry and may bring calamity to the family.

Among the Ao Nagas the elders ot the clan get priority in selection of the plot. After they have made their selection according to their choice the younger ones get their chance (Roy Burman, 1966).

In some areas, for instance among the Chero, the selection of jhum plots is made by lottery and a similar system is followed by the Lushai of Mizoram. Among the Maria of Abujhmar hills the field for shifting cultivation (Penda) is selected by the *patel* or village leader in consultation with Mokaddam and Panchamukhia members of the *de facto* village council. The Maria of Abujhmar hills mark some high trees at the outer line of their agricultural plot and exempt them from felling. These trees form the boundary of one's holding. Among the shifting cultivators of Keonjhar hills also the system of distributing Taila plot is identical to that of the Maria.

The Purum of Manipur choose the plots of land on their own. The plot of agricultural land selected by one from a village is not necessarily adjacent to those selected by others of the same village. They hardly realize the advantages of their plot being adjacent to those of the others from the point of view of protection. After the selection of a particular plot the occupant marks its boundary which is respected by his co-villagers. A dispute over the violation of boundary is decided by Khullakpa (chief officer of the village) with the help of the village elders (Das, 1945).

Among the Dimasa tribe of Assam the dry land is tax free and hence a household can cultivate any amount of land without taking prior approval of the village council. Lands of individual farmers are demarcated either by natural land marks or by placing two wooden sticks crosswise at each corner of the field. This method of marking the land is locally known as *daupher*. A particular plot once selected and demarcated is not encroached upon even if it is left fallow for many years.

In the Garo Hills district of Meghalaya there are a number of legal factors which have a major role in selection of a Jhum plot. Under the Garo Hill district regulation the following types of land cannot be selected and allotted to any person for jhum cultivation or to cut any forest:

a) land within a radius of 40 metres of any water source or catchment area.

b) land within a distance of 50 metres on either side of the state public works department or district council roads.

c) any area covered by sal or other valuable trees and

d) any village or community forest recognised as such under the Garo Hills (Forest) Act, 1958. (Borah and Goswami, 1977).

Among the Angami of north Manipur all the households select the plots only on one side of the village leaving the other side for grazing purposes. The one who selects a plot on the wrong side faces severe difficulty in guarding it against the birds and beasts. Furthermore, he can not claim compensation if his crops are damaged by somebody's cattle.

The Baiga of Madhya Pradesh prefer to keep the *bewar* nearer to cheir residence so that it is more convenient for their wives to carry *pej* (meals) to them. It also enables them to protect the Bewar from wild animals. They can, however, opt for a patch even 3 to 4 kilometres away if other factors are favourable. They usually prefer a patch of dense growth as its vegetation lasts two or three burnings and fertility is not exhausted sooner (Nag, 1958).

Among the Hill Bhuiya of Orissa selection of a patch for shifting cultivation is controlled by the traditional village leadership within the limit of village boundary not touching reserved forest boundary. In a meeting of village elders presided over by the *naika* (secular headman) the area for shifting cultivation is selected in consultation with the Dahuri (priest). The *naika* along with the *dahuri* goes on the spot and allots plots for the family members. The size of the family and number of working adults are taken into account to determine the size of individual plots. Among the Juangs of Keonjhar Hills, Orissa, disputes over distribution of land are common because of shortage of land in proportion to the population.

Methods of shifting cultivation

Clearing and burning:

After the suitable area is selected for cultivation the jungle is cleared by felling the trees and lopping off the undergrowth, using simple tools such as the axe and dao. This operation is conducted during December and January. Among the Bhuiyas it is done during Phalgun-Chaita (i.e. February-March). In Garo Hills the trees are cut 2 to 3 feet (0.6 m to 0.9 m) above the ground. The Maler adopt a similar practice. After the harvest the lower portions of the trees are used as firewood. The fruit trees like mango, Mahua, Khend and Karam are protected from cutting. During the felling several trees are left which are used as boundary pillars between family plots besides being used for several climbing vegetable plants such as beans.

Usually it takes less than a month to clear the whole area allotted for a single family. But, it may exceed a month if the jungle consists of hardwood and no bamboo. The felled trees and bushes are allowed to dry in the sun for about a month. Bamboo takes the least time to dry and the harder the trees the greater the time given for drying. Once the whole plot is cleared then the dried forest is set on fire. In several villages of Keonjhar Hills, apart from *taila* a small terrain is given to another type of cultivation, akin to shifting cultivation, which is known as *Guru.* In addition to the bushes, felled trees sometimes brought from elsewhere are deposited on the field and set alight. Such fields are kept fallow for a much shorter period of four to five years. Occasionally a single firing is not sufficient to burn all the trees; bamboo forests can be reduced by a single firing but hardwood forests require two firings. The fertility of the soil depends on the total deposition of ash on the ground and complete burning helps to produce a better yield. Usually the firing is followed by the spreading of ash on the soil, and in this way the nutrients contained in the vegetation, in particular, calcium, phosphorous, potassium and nitrogen are added to the soil. In the Keonjhar Hills the burning operation is required only in the newly acquired land or first years Taila. In the second year, this field has to be fertilized. Some small bushes which grow during those months after harvesting in addition to some others cut down and brought from nearby forests, are deposited in the centre of each taila field and burnt to ashes. In this way, they replenish soil fertility in the second year.

The shifting cultivators all over India can assume when rainfall will occur and accordingly select the date for firing. People in different regions of India, practising shifting cultivation, have good practical knowledge of the local climate and they make a more or less correct speculation of the time the monsoon will break. They set fire to the dried forest within a few days of the heavy showers that come and distribute and mix the ashes with the soil and increase its fertlity. The burning of debris makes the soil capable of receiving the seed without the preparatory tillage. Further, if the soil is stirred by any implement it gets loose and is likely to suffer from heavy run-off during the rains. In the Garo Hills the burning operation is done in March and the Bhuiyas of Orissa conduct it in Baisakh (April-May).

After firing, a number of tree trunks may remain unburnt and may create difficulties in sowing. Such unburnt wood is removed. In the Garo Hills the unburnt and unwanted logs are collected from the field for erecting fences around the farm or else they are kept aside. Sometimes the logs are kept horizontally on the slopes to prevent soil erosion. The unburnt little tree trunks are collected for fuel. The clearing operation (Aba-Khila) is done in the latter part of March. One or two showers are sufficient to settle down the ash in the field. After the clearing is completed, the field becomes ready for sowing.

Sowing:

The method of sowing seeds under shifting cultivation in different regions is more or less similar. The seeds of millet and chillies are broadcast over the same plot. Seeds of other crops such as paddy, sesamum, gourd and brinjal are sown dibbled in separate holes. Cotton is sown by dibbling by most of the Garos, but some sow it by broadcasting as well. The shifting cultivators like the Juang. Pauri Bhuiya of Orissa, the Angami, Lhota, Rengma and Sema of North Eastern India dig a little hole by dibbling stick and drop the seeds into the hole. The tribles like Ao, Chang and Koya sow by broadcasting.

In shifting cultivation seeds are generally sown in a mixed pattern. The proportion and types of crop mixture depend, by and large, on traditional wisdom which conforms to the soil conditions and climate. In Northeast India the minimum and maximum number of crops in the mixture are found to be three and ten respectively (Borah and Goswami, 1977: 37). In Garo Hills paddy, maize, millet, arum, tapioca, sweet-potato, chilli, different vegetables, sesamum, ginger, cotton and jute are sown in the mixture. The Lushai grow tobacco, chilli and sugarcane in separate plots, cotton is also cultivated separately or else is sown with other crops in the same plot. Among the Juangs, *madia* and *gogoi,* two millets similar to jowar and bajra are cultivated along with the paddy in the border of the fields. The hard and thick stems of these plants form a barrier against wild animals. The Angami usually grow rice in newly cleared jhum plots and millet, maize or jobstear are grown in the second year. Among the Jhumia 50 per cent of the total jhum area under cultivation is used for paddy, 30 per cent for cotton, 15 per cent for sesamum and 5 per cent for vegetables and root crops. Unlike Lushai Hills, seeds in Keonjhar hills are sown in a more systematic way. The central portion of the field is restricted to paddy which is the shortest plant. Encircling the paddy different seeds are selected according, to the size of the crop. In this way paddy, the shortest plant among other crops takes the central position and Madia, the tallest of the crops takes the perimeter of the field.

Seed sowing and planting continues from the end of March to the end of April in the Garo Hills. A mixture of seeds of millet, chilli, brinjal, bean, gourd, and lady's finger is broadcast first. Paddy, maize and cotton seeds are sown in holes dug by dibble stick at appropriate distances. Sowing in holes is done from the lower to upper slopes. After this, arum, tapioca, sweet potato, ginger and banana are planted in the field.

Among the Birjhia, arhar is grown as a common cereal. Cucumber is also a common crop among them. The other crops grown by them are marka and tangun. When the rainy season approaches the Birjhia cultivators broadcast marua seeds all over the plot and then the entire plot is scratched with a land scratcher through which the seeds and the ashes get mixed up and absorb rain water properly.

Crops grown in Swidden cultivation

Shifting cultivation has very little scope for specialization as diverse crops are sown in a single plot of land. Notable among the main crops are paddy, tapioca, millet, maize, jobstear, sweet potato, yam, beans, mustard, turmeric, ginger, brinjal, tomato, pumpkin, gourd, onion, chilli and tobacco. Vegetables like cucumber, chilli, onion, ginger are grown in places where the heaps of woods are burnt and is more fertile due to accumulation of ashes.

Ginger is the main commercial crop of the Abor of Assam. The shifting cultivators of M.P. also grow leafy vegetables, melon, cucumbers, root vegetables and pulses. The Baiga grow arhar in the middle of the Bewar plot and on its boundary lines. They also grow some other crops such as sanwa, mandia, juar and brinjal. Besides the above crops some crops are grown by certain tribes according to their needs. For instance, the Purum of Manipur grow sauki and eat the leaves in addition to cereals.

Among the Juang of the Keanjhar Hills a new *taila* (jhum plot) is used for a cash crop which is primarily russi, an oilseed and birhi a pulse. In the second year *taila* is used for mixed cropping, starting from paddy and millets to beans and pulses. From the third year it is left fallow.

In addition to the above mentioned crops, cotton is grown by the Naga, Garo, Kuki, Reangs and Tripuri and some tribes of Assam. Chillies and vegetables grown by the shifting cultivators of Manipur, Tripura and Nagaland frequently find their way to the market. It has been noted that potato, tomato, and other vegetables and fruit have been introduced in the recent past.

Of what might be called natural crops, among the Angami of north Manipur, the principal is thatching grass, which is of great importance in some villages with little jhum land. It is protected from damage and encroachment, but not otherwise cultivated, and is usually village or clan property.

The crops are generally raised in mixed farming. The usual items are paddy maize, cotton, millet and vegetables of various kinds. Some crops are grown as a single crop. Sesamum is usually a single crop in Mikir Hills, paddy is a single crop in Garo Hills in the second year of cultivation, sugarcane is a single crop in Mizo Hills as well as Mikir Hills. Shifting cultivation has very little scope for specialization as diverse crops are shown in a single plot of land.

Watching the crop:

Crop raising in Jhum cultivation is a strenuous job. Besides the occasional pests and diseases, there is fear of birds, rats and wild animals destroying the crops both during day and night. Parrots, wild cocks, rats, wild bears, porcupines, rabbits, monkeys and occasionally wild elephants are the enemies of crops. In order to save the crops from such enemies, the shifting cultivators in many areas, such as in the Garo Hills, construct watch-houses. The Maler construct temporary watch huts called *khallu kuriya* in the Kurwa field. They also make a high platform known as 'Danda' where they sit during the day. While this enables them to keep birds away they however fail to prevent the damage by insects, pests and locusts. Finding themselves helpless in preventing such troubles they start praying to spirits as they believe that they are due to the anger of spirits. The wild animals damage more than half of their crops. A number of implements are used to kill and scare away the wild animals and birds destroying crops.

Soon after the completion of sowing or sometime during the sowing, jhum plots called 'Penda' among the Marias are fenced by wooden logs and bamboo. This is communal work and all adults join in the construction of a heavy fence along the perimeter of the penda. The cultivators have to watch day and night when the crops are ready for harvest particularly the fields lying within the reach of wild animals from the adjoining forest. The Tangkhul Naga construct their field huts selecting a level place in the centre of the field. In this hut, they take their mid-day meal and stay throughout the agricultural activities of the year. This also works as a suitable guard room for them. However, despite constant vigilance it is not easy to save the crops from the wild animals and birds. This is an important factor for the low productivity of crops in the jhum fields.

Weeding

After the first showers many offshoots from the stumps of the trees come out. Several varieties of grass also grow and if they are not checked they may stifle the growth of the crops and take away the nutrients and water content of the soil. For this reason at least once and generally twice, weeding and cutting of offshoots is practised during the growing period of the crop.

Weeding is one of the most strenuous and labour consuming parts of the shifting cultivation. It is essential in shifting cultivation, as without it the farmers cannot expect to harvest anything from their field. It is a continuous process to tackle the rapid growth of the weeds. Weeding is done solely by human labour. At least four weedings are necessary, otherwise the undergrowth may use up the lion's share of water in the soil (Bose, 1967). Among the Jhumia of Tripura weeding is done at least thrice. It is labour intensive work and it plays a decisive role in the economy of a Jhumia family. Among the Jhumia both men and women take part in weeding and are also joined by their children in this work. Among the Purum also, weeding is usually done three times. Among the Tangkhul Naga weeding is usually done twice in an agricultural year. Sometimes it becomes essential to carry out this operation three times in a year if the weeds grow faster. This is so if the field is cultivated after a short interval and the burning operation is not very successful due to weather conditions.The Mal Paharia make every effort to protect the growing plants against injurious grasses. Normally a Khallu crop is weeded two to three times for yielding rich harvest.

The burning destroys weeds in the Jhum to some extent. This is one of the principal attractions for the tropical cultivators towards shifting cultivation. Weeds grow very fast in the rainfed areas in the tropics. The difficulty of getting the weeding done in time imposes a limit on the area which a family can cultivate.

In Northeast India generally three to four weedings are done. In some cases, as in the case of the Apatani the fields are weeded three to five times depending on the irrigation received. Among most of the shifting cultivator tribes both men and women assisted by their children take part in weeding. In some other areas weeding is the exclusive duty of the women folk. In the Garo Hills weeding in the jhum field is done four times. The first weeding which requires much labour and time is after twenty-five days of sowing the seeds. The rest are in mid June, August, September and in early November. The first three weedings are applicable in case of all crops while the last two weedings are for the long duration crops like cotton and chilli.

It is found that weeding and harvesting go side-by-side. The members of the family who go for weeding bring some ripe products in the basket (*khirang*) on their back while returning home from the field. The cultivators harvest the perishable crops in time and prevent them from rotting in the field.

Harvesting

In shifting cultivation generally there is mixed farming with the harvesting of different crops being done as and when they are ready. The method of harvesting is also a crude one. Sickles are sometimes used for paddy harvesting and in many cases paddy is harvested only by picking by hand and filling a basket on the back. In harvesting root crops like arum, tapioca and ginger where digging is necessary, either a dao or a hoe used.

Among the Lushai, harvesting begins in August. Maize is the first crop to ripen. After maize the fast-growing paddy is harvested in September. Generally, after the busiest season all the harvesting is completed before Christmas. Among the Jhumia paddy is first crop to be harvested in Bhadra Ashwin (September–October), maize is harvested next, followed by sasamum. Cotton is usually the last produce to be plucked off from the Jhum land in the month of

Kartik and Agrahanya (November–December). The different vegetables including cow peas and chillies are harvested frequently from the third month to almost the end of the seasonal calender. Similar is the agricultural calendar of the Idu Mishimi.

Among the Maria the bulk of the harvesting begins in October–November when Kosra ripens. It is followed by the harvest of other varieties of millet. Paddy is harvested in November–December. The remaining crops, mainly the vegetables and pulses are harvested next. Harvesting ends with Idka in January.

The Lushai Hills, specially the southern side, occasionally faces crop failure on account of the cyclones which sweep over the area. Crop failure also occurs in the Lushai hills at intervals of 25 and 50 years. The two kinds of famine locally known as *thingtam* and *mautam* are caused by bamboo. After every 50 years the bamboos start flowering and bearing seed and finally the old generation dies out. This is followed by invasion of rats which devour the rice crop and cause a famine.

Storage

The safe preservation of the produce is a major problem for the farmers. The Garo shifting cultivators dispose a considerable amount of their product soon after harvest. The tuber crops are directly brought from the field for consumption or sale according to requirements. Cotton, the main cash crop, is sold soon after harvest by most of the farmers. Some economically better off families hold back cotton for a few months with the intention of selling at a higher price. A considerable amount of paddy is preserved safely for future consúmption. Besides paddy, millets and maize are also kept in a granary. Vegetables like pumpkin that can be preserved for a longer period are kept either in the kitchen or in the granary.

The Adi and other groups of Mishmi do not store the grains in their houses, but in granaries built at some distance from their houses. This method saves the foodstuff should the house get burnt.

Other varieties of Swidden cultivation

There are some other varieties of Swidden cultivation with some variations. For instance among the Kamars the two other patterns of shifting cultivation besides Dahi are 'Beora' and 'Guhad'. In Beora cultivation trees with a girth of about one and a half feet (46 cm) and more are not felled. In other respects Beora is also identical to Dahi system. Guhad is however, restricted to few villages of Mainpuri and Khariar tract of Raipur district which have an ample supply of Katai bamboo (Dube, 1951: 35). The yield in the guhad field is believed to be unusually large.

The Bhuiya tribe of Orissa practise shifting cultivation with names *Dahi* and *Koman*. In the Dahi method they clear a more or less level patch on a hill slope. All the trees, bushes and shrubs are cut down and left to dry. Once they are dry they are burnt, the land is dug up and rice is planted. In the *Koman* method all the bushes and shrubs are cut and placed in heaps round the trees and they are burnt after a month or two. The fires destroy the branches and twigs leaving the scorched and baked trunks. The ashes are then spread all over the Koman plot. In one part of the Koman plot the upland rice is sown and some other crops in the rest of it. Beans are sown round the tree trunks.

In a pattern called *alda* in Nagaland the tribes cut but do not burn at the time of shifting cultivation. Thus the cut plants and undergrowth grow very quickly the next year with fresh leaves and thus prevent soil erosion and also preserve soil fertility. In many areas in Nagaland tree trunks are used across the slope so as to check the velocity of water. In some areas where the slopes are covered with grass and bamboo groves; pegs, bamboo pieces and grass are fixed across the slope to prevent soil erosion. Through the deposition of washed down soil along the tree trunk or bamboo and grass barriers, a sort of rudimentary terrace develops in the course of time.

Chapter Four

SOCIO-CULTURAL IMPERATIVES

Shifting cultivation has a special significance in the ethos of concerned tribal society and the social relationship, cultural values and mythical belief are directly linked with it. Tribal values orientation is one of the basic causes underlying the continuance of shifting cultivation among most of the tribes of hill regions. In some cases it is observed that the value problem has affected the adoption of settled agriculture where the land is already available or is made available by the government. An instance from a Toto family of west Bengal shows that the adoption of settled paddy cultivation by a son was opposed by his father as the settled agriculture would require preservation of the grain for consumption purposes for a longer duration whereas the father wanted to offer a feast and alcoholic rice beer to those persons who would join him in a reciprocal labour relationship in connection with shifting cultivation (Roy Burman and Sharma, 1970: 154).

There are many other illustrations of how value and traditional concepts appear as obstacles to the introduction of improved agricultural practices among the tribals. In the study of the Toto it has been observed that certain varieties of millets are symbolically associated with their community life. They would not cultivate the varieties which exist among the neighbouring Nepalis, for it would be considered to be almost moral apostasy. Similarly, the Nepalis would not cultivate the varieties cultivated by Totos because they consider the latter to be culturally low.

The Baigas do not use a plough because they do not want to tear the breast of mother earth. This is the making of the Baiga shifting cultivators as settled cultivators. The Mizo and the Garo too have remained shifting cultivators though they do not harbour any such belief. The Mizo however prefer hill-top settlements. In the past it was because they wanted protection from infectious diseases prevailing among the valley dwellers. Though the cause no longer remains there, they continue to stay on hill tops. A section of Mizas has settled in the plains but it is quite small in number.

For the Koyas *Podu* cultivation is not a mere set of agricultural practices, it contains a whole nexus of Kaya religious beliefs, attitudes, self image and tribal identity. Among them there are three cycles of ritual. One is associated with disease, another with phratry and clan and a third with Podu cultivation. In such a network it is quite natural for a Koya to believe that those who still practise *podu* cultivation are practicipating in something that is an essential component of Keya life. To the Koya, the *bhumi talli* (earth-mother) is inhabited by unseen forces whose powers influence man's destiny. They control the rains, the fertility of crops, the vigour and health of men and animals, and they can always be found burning somewhere in the vicinity of every piece of luck and each misfortune. The Koya believe that the earth goddess demands offering in return for beautiful harvests, vigorous livestock, healthy humans and successful hunting parties. Koyas beg her permission before harvesting any crop, cutting trees, hunting or tilling the soil. The first share of every major crop and a portion of all the animals slain are offered to mother earth. They believe that the mother earth is fond of blood and lusts for animal sacrifice. As the belief exists blood imparts fertility and stirs the earth into frenzies of reproduction and every ceremony dedicated to 'Bhumi talli' must include the sacrifice of at least a chiken. In the pre-British period even human offerings were made to 'bhumi talli' once a year. Even today many Koyas believe that human sacrifice (narabali) is still offered to bhumi talli in the remote hills (Tyler, 1974: 23).

The Koya is fully guided by mythical belief in conducting agricultural operation. Before cutting the growth or a particular plot the Koya would see whether any strange, unexplained events occur in its vicinity. Then the final decision is taken after a dream. Should he dream of white cloth, cows, elephants or horses (that is domesticated animals) the signs are considered to be favourable and he will proceed to the next step but should he dream of black cloth, pigs, tigers or jackals or dead people, he will abandon the site and proceed to an alternate plot subjecting it to the same tests as the previous one. A similar dominance of mythical belief and the role of dreams is found among the Lakher.

For the Garo the *jhum* cultivation constitutes the pivot of their social life. It is observed with due solemnity and much eclat. Worship of dieties is calculated to bring prosperity and bumper crops. The chain of rites and rituals of the Garo begins with Agalmoka or Achiroka which is observed to invoke rains. The Jamegapa-aha-u-a is observed at the time of sowing seeds. In this, boiled grains of paddy are offered to the god of harvest who can save the crop for the year. In mangela celebration each of the family prays to god with offerings of jhum produce from their own land. This is observed after harvest.

Among the Soliga, observance of rites are necessary before final selection. Even in these settlements which were once cultivated, the Soliga have to go in for *hundeya* and consequent rituals have to be observed. Dreams form the basis for final decision. The results of the dreams of elders living during the *hundeya* cumulatively lead them to decide whether to form a podu or not.

Thus for most of the shifting cultivators their mode of agriculture is a way of life. All elements in social living are geared to and integrated into the continued operation of culture on this level. The different stages of jhum operation are connected with agricultural rites and ceremonies. The adoption of new techniques of agriculture may not provide facilities to worship the appropriate dieties. The shift from traditional type of cultivation means partial shift from their traditional way of life itself. Hence the introduction of settled cultivation among the tradition-bound shifting cultivators will be a long process because it will contain in itself the seed of a vital change in their lives.

Rites and rituals connected with swidden cultivation

Rites and rituals constitute an integral part of the shifting cultivation economy. At various stages of shifting cultivation we find the initiation through various rites and rituals. These activities are integrated with the tribal belief and socio-cultural life.

The Konyak do not perform any rite or ceremony till the beginning of sowing but once the seed is embedded in the earth they realise the threat of nature and solicit protection of god by offerings and prayers. At the first ceremonial sowing the founder of the village sacrifices a chicken in one of his fields on behalf of the whole village and offers it to the sky-god *gowang*.

The Lakher who decide about the selection of a particular agriculture plot through dreams have *ria long chtri* sacrifices as the first ritual related to shifting cultivation. Leaving the jhum half cut all the plot owners gather to celebrate the *ria long chtri*. The day after the sacrifice is known as *aoh* and is a day for complete rest, no work is done on this day at all. After the cutting operation is completed all those having jhums on a particular slope bring their beer to the house of one of their members for a feast.

Among the Idu Mishmi a sacrifice is usually performed before the sowing of seeds to ensure a good crop. A fowl is sacrificed and offered to god *Malo,* who is believed to give good crops.

Among the Purum the worship of Nungchungba marks the beginning of the agricultural operation of the year. When the paddy stalks appear usually by the month of Mera (October–November) the worship of Sabuhog is performed. A Purum householder begins his harvest only after the first fruits of the year are offered to Se-namahi by his *pipa* (head of the Sib or subsib officiating as the priest).

In the Keonjhar Hills the *tritia* festival is found to be observed before sowing begins. This ceremony is observed on the third day of the new moon in the month of Baisakh (April–May). In this ceremony some seeds of paddy are transferred from the hut to the jungle. This signifies the belief that if a demon comes in the form of property and agriculture, Lakshmi may be transferred to the jungle. After a few days the actual *pudhan* or *buita* with the help of village committee and other elders brings the pot containing paddy seeds from the tree implying that the demon is already driven out and the goddess Lakshmi has come to the village. The goddess is received by the villagers with drums and music and is placed upon a specially erected platform near *gramsiri* (village god). Later on these seeds are used as sacred seeds during sowing.

Among the Pauri Bhuiya there are two important rituals performed on threshing ground known as *gundamanda* and *khala puja,* on *khala puja* we find a direct impact of Hindu rituals. In this form of ritual the Hindu goddess of wealth is worshipped with a sacrifice of white chicken and *baram,* the tribal deity, with another chicken.

The Juang perform *gundadia* ritual on their respective fields offering shares of their product to the local dieties and to their ancestors.

The Kamar use the services of the local *baiga* to start the burning operation of *dahi* plot. The Baiga prays to the *budharaja* for protection of crops and better yield.

Among the Maler the series of rituals begins right before sowing. Before the seeds are sown, the Maler offer a chicken or an egg to *dade gossain* (the god of the Kurwa forest) and promise to offer him a goat or a pig whichever he would require provided the harvest be a bumper one. This busy and complex agricultural operation is followed by festivals of music and dance. These festivals and merry-making depend upon the success of the Kurwa. The most important festival of the Maler known as *pelai* is observed when the crops are harvested and stored. This festival is associated with worship of different gods and the ancestors. It is a festival of both joy and sorrow. Joy is associated with the meeting of relatives living far and wide. The sorrow is associated with the memory of the dead ancestors. The Maler propitiate the different gods and goddesses along with dead ancestors as not to harm the family and to protect the village from epidemic. The meeting of the different village people leads to the selection of the bride and groom and the meeting of the lover and beloved. It is observed that if the yield is beautiful the festival is observed with full fanfare and even a buffalo is sacrificed. The buffalo sacrifice is known as 'Managarme' among them. The relatives, gathered together on the eve of Managarme, are offered Taadi (maize beer or Bajra beer) followed by the feast if the yield is bumper. If the yield is meagre they are offered simply *taadi.* Thus *khallu* is the hub round which the life of the Meler revolves. It is central because it provides them the maize on which they subsist. It has religious import because the moral and religious system is determined by it. The sacredness of their life is reflected in the sanctions and taboos associated with the Khallu operation. According to the existing belief among Maler a moral man is one who works on Khallhu land, offers sacrifices to the Gossaiyan and observes all the taboos and customs associated with Khallu cultivation.

The Koya carefully preserve the grain from productive and vigorous plants and use it as seed for the new year's crop. Before sowing, a handful of each kind of seed to be seen in the coming year is taken from the storage baskets and handed over to the village priest who sprinkles them after mixing in some of the blood from animals sacrificed in a village ceremony dedicated to the mother earth (bhumi talli). When he receives the impregnated seeds from the priest, the cultivator takes them to his field and after saluting the mountain goddess sows them in a corner. The rest of the seeds are sown following the initiation ceremony.

Brief cultural profile of swidden societies

1. The Purum

The Purum tribe is one of the old Kuki tribes of Manipur. Its members live on the western fringe of the hills that separate the hills of Manipur from the Kabaw valley. The Purum people were earlier wrongly described as a clan but it was later found that they were a distinct tribe. They are endogamous and are known by a specific name. They have a dialect of their own and claim a specific habitat. Five clans have been identified among them. Each clan is further divided into sub-clans whose headmen are known as *pipa.* The clan is an exogamous organization. A person has to marry from only one or specially selected clans. The Purum live in nuclear families. To raise one's social rank a person has to perform the *genna* sacrifice in which a *mithun* is killed in the course of an elaborate three day ritual. Each village has a headman known as *khulapa* and seven other functionaries. There is a village council known as *ruishang* which deals with all kinds of complaints. Death, mutilation, slavery, ostracism and fine are forms of punishment awarded to guilty persons according to the enormity of their crime. The Purum worshop their ancestral spirits. Their most important duty is *nungchungba.* Nowadays, they have taken to the worship of Hindu deities like Krishna, Rama, Mahadeva, Durga and Kali.

Although shifting cultivation is their major occupation, wet cultivation is not unknown to them. However, wet cultivation is confined to the richer section of the tribe. The shifting cultivation land is owned by the community but the wet valley land is now equally divided among the sons with the youngest getting a slightly larger share.

2. The Dimasa

The Dimasa constitute one of the Kachari tribes of Assam and are concentrated in the United Mikir and Kachar Hills. Since 1961, they have been recognized as a separate tribe. Their population is near about 250,000. The most unique feature of the Dimasa social structure is the system of double descent. Both patrilineal and matrilineal systems of descent are in vogue. A man reckons his descent from his paternal grandfather while a woman does so through her maternal grandmother. They are two co-existing and intersecting sibs of kin groups – one matrilineal and the other patrilineal. The kinship terminology is bilateral, generational and determined by mainly sex and seniority and the degree of affinity. Among the Dimasa, nuclear families predominate. They are strictly monogamous. Marriage takes place when a person becomes adult. Bride-price has to be paid. They have a youth dormitory for boys which becomes particularly active at the time of annual harvest festival. Besides this, the dormitory responds to the call of the headman in rendering such social services as tilling the land of an invalid or roofing the house of a widow. The house is inherited by the youngest son. The daughters inherit the mothers' property. The Dimasa worship a number of area deities besides an all-creator God, called 'Madai'. Their most important gods known as Shivaria, and Rama Chandi which correspond to the Hindi gods as Shiva and Kali. Nowadays the worship of Lakshmi and Saraswati has also become common. The village headman known as Khunang among the Dimasa is the oldest living man in the village. The other village offices also go strictly on the principle of seniority of age.

3. The Garo

The Garo are one of the well known tribes of Northeastern India. They live in small agricultural villages of 10 to 50 or 60 houses with a population which rarely exceeds 300. Traditionally, the Garo have lived by swidden cultivation but during the last fifty years, an increasing number of small valley areas have been brought under wet cultivation. Where land is used for permanent cultivation, it is used almost exclusively for wet rice, mustard and jute. But shifting cultivators plant a wide assortment of crops such as rice, millet, maize, cotton, ginger and chilli. The villages consist of a number of substantial bamboo family houses together with associated granaries, timber sheds and pig stys. The Garo are a matrilineal people and belong to five exogamous clans. Each village is the seat of at least one local lineage of one of the matrilineal clans. Though the village is built with the matrilineal discent groups, it is not organised exclusively around a group of co-resident related men or co-resident women. Most frequently a man lives in the village of his wife.

Traditionally the head of the family is a woman and she holds all the property. However the husband can use his wite's possessions. Property goes from mother to daughter. If there is more than one daughter in the family, the mother selects the *nakna* (heiress) who inherits the property. The younger daughter goes away from the family to establish a separate family unit. The maternal uncle has a respectable position since he looks after his sister's family. He has the same role as that of a father in a patrilineal family. In many cases, ne of his sister's sons marries his own daughter. The village headman is known as *nokma.* He is assisted by a council known as *jingmachangge.*

4. The Hill Maria

The Hill Maria reside in the north-western part of the Bastar district of Madhya Pradesh, in the region known as 'Abujhmar'. Their total population is roughly 12,000. The density of population is a little more than nine persons to a square mile (2.6 sq km). In villages that are inhabited only by the Hill-Maria, the population never exceeds 50. Ideally every Hill Maria family should be an extended family. Even if a son breaks away at marriage he will co-operate with the natal family in the pursuit of agricultural tasks. The father and son share a common granary. In each village, there is a youth dormitory known as *ghotul.* There are no age-grades and no formal initiation rites. The dormitory provides a setting for numerous social interactions among adolescent boys of all families regardless of kinship. Hill Maria clans are unilineal descent groups. Each has a name and a particular clan god known as *pen.* Although village exogamy is not prescribed, in effect it works like that. The village headman is known as the 'Patel'. He is the spokesman for all the village when dealing with outside authority beyond that which his own personality and powers of persuasion permit him to exert. There is no formally constituted village council but the elders of the village customarily gather at day break in the youth dormitory.

5. The Angami Naga

The Angami are one of the most important Naga tribes. A large section of these tribes lives by shifting cultivation. Besides, Jhum cultivation, hunting and collection of forest produce gives them some extra income. In addition to rice, they grow maize, beans, oilseeds, mustard, cotton and jute. They make good and strong cloth on tension looms with attractive designs. Basket-making, blacksmithy and wood carving are also popular in the area.

The Angami village is invariably built either on a hilltop or on the ridge of a spur running down from a high range. Each village is fortified with stiff stockades, deep ditches and massive stone walls. Although the village is the unit for the organisation of political and religious aspects of Angami life, the clan is no less important. A man cannot leave his property to any person outside his kindred. Only males can permanently inherit real property. Generally the father divides the bulk of his property during his life time. On the death of the father, the youngest son inherits all the property including the house. Among the Angani, there are a number of beliefs which govern the relationship with the supernatural. The word *kenna* is used in the sense of prohibition or the taboo. It may refer not only to breach of strict social rules but even to that of common usage. While *kenna* is the prohibition laid on a persons' action, *penna* is the prohibition laid on the whole community. They observe a number of festivals know as *genna,* each of which has a specific objective. They have a system of village chiefs who dispense justice and in the past used to lead head hunting raids on other villages. The youth dormitory is insignificant among the Angami. It is used only on ritual occasions and as an occasional sleeping house for youth.

6. The Juang

The Juang are one of the major tribes of Orissa inhabiting the Keonjhar hills. They live in compact settlements. The houses of individual families are built around the 'Majang' or the dormitory house. Close kin tend to build their houses adjacent to each other. Shifting cultivation is the main source of livelihood of the Juang. Some of the Juang are acquainted with lowland paddy cultivation. They supplement their meagre agricultural produce by hunting and the collection of fruits, roots and firewood in the forest. The youth dormitory is an active organization. Its members are divided into a number of age-grades. The dormitory provides a number of services for people of all age-groups. It has its social, economic, political and magico-religious uses for the Juang. The Juang believe in a number of gods and goddesses, some of whom are benevolent. They have distinct deities at the village level, family spirits, deified heroes and mythical characters. Besides these, a number of Hindu deities like Mahadeva, Parvati, Lakshmi, Durga, Rama and Sita are also worshipped. The village leader is known a *nagam, boita* or *dihuri.* He is assisted by a number of assistants. There is also a village council which settles local disputes and punishes transgression of social rules. The Juang has also an inter-village organization which serves as a court of appeal for the verdict of the village panchayat.

7. The Baiga

The Baiga live in the Balaghat, F pur and Mandla districts of Madhya Pradesh. The tribe is strictly endogamous but admit women and other tribes on certain conditions. The Baiga is divided into seven sections or *jat* which occupy separate areas. Each section is also endogamous, and is divided into a number of clans or *got* which are exogamous. Marriage takes place when a person becomes an adult. Payment of bride price is essential. They worship a number of deities which differ from area to area. The principal god is *Buradeo. Thakurdeo* is the god of the village and its boundaries. *Dulhadeo* averts diseases and accident. Besides this *Dhartimata* is also worshipped. A Baiga village is built either in the shape of a circle, a square or a rectangle. The number of huts in a village does not exceed 20 or 25. Since the Baigas are constantly on the move, they do not think of building permanent houses. The Baiga has an eye for a good site. It is either a hill top or an inaccessible forest clearing or the bank of a perennial stream. The village has a well defined boundary near which the burial or cremation ground is located. The Baiga have strongly opposed efforts to wean them from swidden cultivation by the government for more than a hundred years. Part of their subsistence comes from the forest. Fruit, flowers, leaves, roots and tubers supplement their food resources. The Baiga are fond of cattle.

8. The Kamar

The Kamar are a small tribe of a little over 10,000 people. They inhabit the Dhamtari Tehsil of Raipur district in Madhya Pradesh. The Kamar settlement is very small and comprises four to twenty families. The existing subdivisions in the tribe are territorial and not endogamous. The tribe is divided into seven clans called *got.* The Kamar are patrilineal and patrilocal. They are extremely individualistic in their social life. Kamar society is unstratified. They do not have a system of a tribal chief or even a territorial chief. However, a number of tribal settlements come together to form a Panchayat. The head of the Panchayat is the *kurha.* But it is a Sarpanch who dispenses justice. The Kamar practise three different forms of shifting cultivation, namely, Dahi, Beora, and Guhad. Besides this, there is another practice known as Pharha which is a half way house between shifting and settled plough cultivation. Near their fields, they would cut down half a dozen trees and branches of larger trees, burn them and prepare a seedbed with the ashes. When the plants grow to one and a half feet (46 cm), they are transplanted in the regular fields. Besides shifting cultivation, the Kamar supplement their resources through hunting for which they have a good reputation. Fishing, collection of honey, mahua flowers, chiraunji and edible roots and leaves are also resorted to. Some of the Kamars are also expert in basket making. Some people supplement their livelihood by wage labour particularly with forest contractors. The Kamar worship several categories of gods and deities. The cult of *gata-dooma* i.e. Mata and the ancestral spirit are universal. Besides these, goddesses of diseases are also propitiated. They have now begun to worship such Hindu gods as Mahadeva – Bhagwan and Hanuman.

9. The Maler

The Maler are one of the largest tribes practising shifting cultivation in India. They number more than fifty thousand and inhabit the Sahebgunj, Pakur and Godda subdivisions of the Santhal Parganas district in Bihar. They speak a language which is closely related to the intermediate Dravadian language family. They do not have any clans among them. The lineage or *byare* is considered an important unit of social interaction. They still have the youth dormitory known as Koddada. The unmarried boys and girls of the village meet there every evening. It is there that they get training in tribal custom, traditional occupations and music and dance. The Maler village is a small cluster in which the number of families varies between 14 to 27. The villages are situated on steep hill slopes or hilltops. The settlements give an appearance of neatness or orderliness. Each settlement has a series of sacred centres marked by either stones or wooden pillars or trees or groves. The sacred centres are the abode of different Gossaiyan or deities. The deities are worshipped by the traditional sacred specialists called Manjhiye. The entire social system of the Maler is interwoven with their dominant occupation, *khallu* cultivation. The various deities and spirits have also been assigned specific roles in making the agricultural yield bountiful. So strong is this interaction that the Maler have constantly refused to be settled on the foot hills in permanent plough fields. The Maler have an elaborate system of social control. They village headman known as *manjhiye* is assisted by a number of functionaries. Above a number of villages, there is the divisional headman known as the Sardar. The Maler are one of the poorest tribes in the country. Living as they do in inaccessible areas, the pace of development is extremely slow.

10. The Koya

The Koya are one of the Dravidian speaking tribes of South Orissa. They are found in the Malkangiri subdivision of Koraput district. Koya villages lie in the midst of forest clearings. Most villages can only be approached by narrow footpaths in the forest. The village sites with their surrounding land and forests are said to belong to the founders' clan. There are ten to thirty houses in each village. At the centre of the village is the dancing ground. Most Koya families are joint and comprise members belonging to three generations. Monogamy is the general rule but polygyny is allowed. The Koya make a distinction between consanguineal and affinal kin. Koya society is divided into five phratries. Each phratry is further subdivided between clans. Leadership both political and social is concentrated in the hereditary headman of the village. He takes all the important decisions not only in secular matters but also in religious matters. His office is hereditary. There is no formal village panchayat but the headman takes the advice of elders. He also sits as a member of the clan panchayat even though he may not belong to that particular clan. Headmen of five villages constitute the Mutha Panchayat which decides disputes of a serious nature or those involving people of several villages. Their original belief system centres round the cult of the earth and cult of the village. In all religious ceremonies, the Bhumata and Gudimata are invariably worshipped. The deities are propitiated by the village priest or Perma. The Koya have now added to their pantheon a number of Hindu gods and goddesses. They derive the bulk of their subsistence from shifting cultivation. They supplement their resources by herding cows and bullocks. The possession of cattle wealth gives status to a man in Koya society.

Chapter Five

GOVERNMENT POLICY AND CONSEQUENT DEVELOPMENTS

Shifting cultivation acts as a severe constraint to the rise above the bare minimum level of subsistence for the people who practise it. Furthermore, the carrying capacity of land is limited. These and various other problems related to shifting cultivation have drawn the attention of the central government and also of the state government from time to time. In course of time a number of steps were taken by the central and state governments to better the socio-economic life of the shifting cultivators.

The Indian Forest Act of 1927 laid down that shifting cultivation was subject to control, restriction and abolition by the state government. N.L. Bor, Forest Botanist in the Forest Research Institute, Dehradun, at the Indian Science Congress, 1942, attributed soil erosion in Assam to the practice of shifting cultivation. The Government introduced legislative measures for protection of forests most probably without giving serious considerations to different problems involved in such measures, particularly how it would affect the forest dwellers. The preservation of the flora and fauna of the country and the revenue derived from the forest products was their focal point. The other important aspect of the measure arising out of the adoption of such an act, that is the proper rehabilitation of the forest people involved in shifting cultivation, was entirely left out of any serious consideration. As a result of this the people involved in it suffered physical and cultural set backs. For such tribes whose social and economic organization is based on food gathering it was detrimental. Once a certain area was declared a reserve by the special power the people dwelling there were ordered to quit the land immediately. Thus, the parts of the forest being declared reserve virtually pushed the shifting cultivator to the plains. Since the plain lands were already under the possession of others the refugees had to settle on lands rejected as unsuitable for agricultural purposes.

The policy adopted by independent India however, appears to have a rational and practical approach. The National Forest Policy of 1952 took a more humane approach to the problem of shifting cultivation.

> The damage caused to forest by shifting cultivation in certain areas must be guarded against. To wean the aborigines who eke out a precarious living from area cultivation, moving from area to area away from their old and wasteful practices, requires persuasion not coercion, a missionary not an authoritarian approach.

In 1953, M.D. Chaturvedi, the then Inspector General of Forests to the Government of India concluded that, 'The notion widely held that shifting cultivation is responsible in the main for large-scale soil erosion needs to be effectively dispelled.'

M.S. Sivaraman, the then Adviser, Programme Administration of the Planning Commission of Government of India observed that:

> It is a mistake to assume that shifting in itself is unscientific land use. Actually it is a practical approach to certain inherent difficulties in preparing proper seed beds in steep slopes where any disturbance of the surface by hocing and ploughing will result in washing away the fertile topsoil. The tribal people therefore take care not to plough or disturb the soil before sowing. The destruction of weeds and improvement of tilth necessary for a proper seed bed are achieved with the help of fire. In most of the interior areas where communication is not developed and sufficient land suitable for terracing is not available, Jhuming alone can be done for the present and as such every effort should be made to improve the fertility of the jhumed land. (Roy Burman and Sharma, 1970,: 152).

The government of the State and Union Territories of the country are aware of the dangers of shifting cultivation and they have taken various measures for the control of shifting cultivation. The system and rules of control on shifting cultivation by the forest authorities vary from state to state. One of the measures taken in this direction is to provide colonies for settled cultivation and subsidies for the purchase of cattle, tools, implements and seeds. Financial help is also given for housing, medical and education facilities.

In order to avoid the harmful effects of shifting cultivation and to get better yields from permanent cultivation on the hill-slopes by applying modern technology, contour bunding and terraces have been devised. Most of the state governments have recognized the importance of the means to be adopted for dealing with the problems of shifting cultivation. A number of approaches have been taken in this regard. These range from relatively obvious remedies such as terraced cultivation to relatively innovative schemes such as rubber and coffee plantations, cultivation of cashew nuts, cardamom, black pepper and fruit. However, it has been observed that except for Garo and Mikir hills district it has not yielded fruitful results elsewhere.

Stated below are the important steps taken in jhum control and improvement in the socio-economic life of the shifting cultivators: (i) jhumia colonization; (ii) regrouping of tribal villages; (iii) introduction of terrace cultivation on the hill slopes; and (iv) providing subsidies and introduction of other measures for the betterment in the life condition of the shifting cultivators such as horticulture and taungiya.

Colonization

The colonization scheme was adopted by a number of states. Considerable effort in this direction has been made in Tripura. Orissa, Bihar and Andhra Pradesh.

The Government of Tripura introduced colonization to bring improvement in socio-economic life of the Jhumia. In this scheme the government provided land for settlement and a grant of Rs.500* to each shifting cultivator household and houses or house building grants are given for settlement in a colony established by the administration.

In Tripura it has been observed that the colonization has not succeeded to any notable extent in eradicating the practice of shifting cultivation. There are a number of reasons given for this problem. These could be enumerated as follows:

* Approximately 9.80 Indian Rupees (Rs) = one United States dollars.

i) The land provided in these colonies is mostly dry land without facilities for irrigation. This actually does not secure good crops.

ii) In many colonies, the forest department did not release the land even after the tribals came to live there.

iii) The reclamation subsidy and the grant for purchase of agricultural equipment were not always made available in time.

iv) After moving over to the colonies the tribals lacked the means to support themselves till the next crop was raised. In the very first year they grew some crops but in subsequent years the yields became poorer leading to dejection among the settlers, as a result of which they lost interest in settled life and reverted to the traditional one.

v) The physical structure of the houses in the colonies are often not suitable for the social and cultural needs of the tribals.

vi) Where the tribals in a colony are brought together from different areas, they find that their manners and customs are incompatible and therefore it is difficult for them to live together.

Furthermore, it was also found that the tribal households bifurcated to take advantage of the scheme and at the same time maintain the old way of life. These households took possession of the houses allotted to them but did not abandon the houses in the old habitats. The household was geographically bifurcated, its economy was one. Thus the house in the colony proved to be only an additional shelter for them and not a substitute for their home on the hill. (Dar, 1970: 187).

In Orissa during the past two decades a number of colonies have been established in the tribal areas to divert the shifting cultivators to settled agriculture by providing cultivable land, necessary inputs and residential accommodation. A study conducted by Tribal and Harijan Research-cum-Training Institute in 1960 revealed that in certain colonies the tribals are engaged as agricultural and hired labourers although the purpose of the colonization scheme was the administrative inability to make available irrigational facilities and other inputs in time. Agricultural extension programmes were also not organized to orient the tribal farmer toward the agricultural practice with which he was not acquainted.

In 1954 the Government of Bihar launched a scheme for the geographical rehabilitation of the Maler, in persuasion of which the Malër were encouraged to come down to the valleys where they could take to plough and settled agriculture. This scheme was launched to check the widespread destruction of forest under shifting cultivation and bring the shifting cultivators closer to modern farming. This was the major objective with which the government of Bihar launched the resettlement scheme of Pararkola in 1954 which was followed by Kunda Pahar, Dumarchir and Murgabani colonies in 1959.

The above scheme had to face the strong resistance of the Maler shifting cultivators who in no manner agreed to settle down to the plains and hence due to this strong opposition the resettlement scheme was abandoned by the Government of Bihar. Some of the major reasons for the opposition on the part of the shifting cultivators were as follows: Firstly, they are already well settled in the forest economy and feared that they would not have the alternative means of subsistence on the plains which they can easily have on the hills. Secondly, the slash and burn cultivation is the pivot of their economy and their rites, rituals and moral order revolve round it. They do not want to disturb the order thus set. They are of the belief that their spirits and 'gossaiyans' are settled in and around the village on the hills, which ought to be worshipped in response to the tradition of the hill culture. Fourthly, the Maler have developed a pattern of the social life of Maler including sexual behaviour which they think possible in their forest habitat. Fifthly, due to their historical animosity and hostility towards the Santhal the Maler refrain from settling down to the valleys. (Vaidyarthi, 1975: 324).

In order to avoid hardship to the Soliga shifting cultivators the then Mysore Government launched a scheme to settle them in a tribal colony near the temple village (Biligiri Rangana temple) in 1963 but the scheme did not meet with success as the tribals wanted to retain their settlements in the interior forest environment.

A study of the impact of colonization on the tribes of Andhra

Pradesh reveals that it has not been successful in wearing away the tribes from 'Podu' cultivation because of the following reasons:

First of all there was a persistent communication gap between the local agencies of the government and the tribal colonists. The colonists could not understand the main aim of the government. They expected that the foodgrains, clothing and considerable sums of money provided to them on account of forest reclamation would continue for a long time. The governments' planning of the housing and settlement did not appear to be in conformity with the tribal requirements. The traditional type of long houses, which were the source of co-operation among them were done away with. It was also difficult for one tribal group to get closer to another alien group settled with them in the colonization scheme.

Regrouping the village

The Soil Conservation Department of the Government of Meghalaya prepares land for permanent cultivation. The land prepared is handed over to the Nokma (village headman) of the concerned Akhing to distribute among his villagers at the rate of two hectares per family, Seeds, manure and fertilizers required for cultivation in the initial years of free cost are provided by the department. Besides these the Garo cultivations are also provided irrigation facilities for permanent cultivation. To enable them to shift from jhum areas to far off places for permanent cultivation, they are provided a house construction grant at the rate of Rs.2,000 per family. The package programme is taken up by combining smaller hamlets into a bigger unit. All such bigger units thus built are linked by motorable road. The villages in catchment areas or those on ground too steep for agricultural purpose are taken up for afforestation and cash crops. Furthermore, drinking water facilities are being provided for each settled village. In the period 1974-76, 1346 jhum cultivator families benefitted under the soil conservation scheme in Meghalaya (Borah and Goswami, 1977: 46).

As a measure to control shifting cultivation the Government of Tripura also took a similar step. Under this scheme the Jhumia were given land and a house construction grant. Data available indicates that between the year 1953-54 to 1967-68 about 20,595 families were settled on 77,076 acres (30,830 ha) (Dar, 1970: 187).

Terrace cultivation

It has been observed that some tribes have traditionally nurtured skills for constructing terraces. Faultless terraces have been built using minimal tools. Hill springs have been used for irrigation. Traditional paddy grown without modern inputs in these areas has provided a greater yield comparable to those on the plains under similar conditions. Hence, some states, particularly Meghalaya have proposed terracing as an alternative to jhuming. Terraces are constructed by the soil conservation department.

In Meghalaya, terrace construction for settled cultivation was encouraged since the establishment of the soil conservation department in 1957-58. Initially a subsidy at the rate of 80 per cent towards the cost of terracing and reclamation was given to the cultivators in cash. Later on the cash subsidy was totally abandoned as it did not work satisfactorily. But it has been found that the terrace land under subsidy schemes was not utilized continuously.

The density of population in the rural areas of Meghalaya is 39 persons per sq km while the average carrying capacity of land under shifting cultivation in the hill region is 4-6 persons per sq km. The Government of Meghalaya through the Soil Conservation Department took effective steps for protecting the land and soil and for providing permanent cultivable land to enable the farmers to cultivate and draw benefit from a permanent place. With this perspective, the Meghalaya Government decided to establish some settlements, providing good and clean drinking water, laying down useful and planned roads and other modern amenities that lead to shaping of sound and progressive communities.

Terrace cultivation has been introduced in Meghalaya by the Department of Soil Conservation under the jhum control scheme. During the period 1974-76 altogether 1914 hectares of land were terraced at a cost of Rs. 51.58 lakhs* (Borah and Goswami, 1977: 42). There is also a provision to cover many areas under this scheme. In a study it was revealed that the total cost of resettlement of a family over the three years would be about 11,000. Terraced paddy

* a *lakh* is one hundred thousand.

was expected to yield a minimum of 1,500 kilograms per hectare as against the maximum jhum yield of 600 to 700 kilograms. (Gupta and Sambrani, 1978: 5). Besides terracing, a number of other measures of land improvement are also taken under the *jhum* control scheme such as reclamation, afforestation, irrigation, drinking water facilities and link roads.

The main objectives of introducing terrace cultivation in the hill areas are to save the soil from erosion and to provide the shifting cultivators with permanent cultivable land. It is expected that production of crops, particularly paddy under terrace cultivation, if done in improved method would be much higher than that under shifting cultivation.

In many regions subsidies are given by the Government to persuade the tribals to take to terrace cultivation or wet cultivation. It is however, found that even the grant of subsidies could not make much headway in introducing terrace or wet cultivation. In the study conducted in Nagaland the following reasons were given by the people for the lack of response to the scheme (Roy Burman and Sharma, 1970: 153):

i) The nature of the terrain is not suitable for wet or terrace cultivation;

ii) Plots of cultivation are small and scattered and there is the fear that wild animals will consume them;

iii) Difficulty in making roads linking scattered and far off plots for wet cultivation;

iv) Difficulty in constructing irrigation channels from deep rivers; and

v) Lack of sufficient funds for irrigation.

Furthermore, the villagers also held the view that in the first three years after construction of terrace, the yield is not sufficient enough to meet even their basic necessities. Hence, only those people who are prepared to live a life of austerity for few years for the sake of future prosperity can take to terrace cultivation.

However, evaluation studies undertaken by various organizations and researchers have shown that these efforts have not been very successful everywhere. The major reasons found are: Firstly, the seedlings are not looked after very well. Secondly, these crops take three to five years to bear fruit and bring in cash. The farmers do not have the capacity of support themselves in the interim period, and finally, in most areas the people have remained sceptical about the scheme. It seems that it was introduced without adequate psychological preparation.

In Manipur the tribals have got the right of jhuming even in protected forest areas. The government of Manipur has also provided incentives to the shifting cultivators for adopting terrace cultivation and bringing further improvement in it. Marketing facilities and road and communication are not properly available in this area. The Government of Manipur has taken stock of the situation and taken effective measures to improve the road communication.

Provision of subsidies and other measures

The state and union territories carved out of Assam such as Manipur, Nagaland, Meghalaya, Tripura and also Arunachal Pradesh and Mizoram are expediting the measures to control shifting cultivation and take other soil conservation measures. The area of shifting cultivation is being gradually reduced. The jhum control scheme is like a package programme and includes land development, provision of inputs like seeds and fertilizer, cost of cultivation for the initial years, provision of irrigation facilities, help towards construction of dwelling houses, drinking water facilities and link roads. The scheme of jhum control is being operated under the aegis of States and Union Territories.

The Government of Meghalaya in Collaboration with I.C.A.R. Research complex for North-Eastern Region, shillong has taken up a programme to collect information on the following items:

1. Loss of top soil and fertility due to shifting cultivation;
2. Various crops and soil loss;
3. Suitability of different types of terraces; and
4. Effect of shifting cultivation on water regimes.

It is hoped that with the help of the findings and recommendations given by the Research Complex, the Soil Conservation Department of Meghalaya would take up effective measures for the solution of the Chronic and complex problem of shifting cultivation.

Steps have also been taken to control shifting cultivation by changing land use pattern.

In Assam the following steps have been undertaken:

i) Cash crops. A number of nurseries of cash crops have been started such as those of cashewnuts, black pepper, coffee and cardamom. The quality of coffee produced in Mikin hills and North Cachar hill district is reported to be a superior quality. Arrangements have also been made to distribute such cash crops to the local farmers.

ii) A number of afforestation centres have been opened.

iii) Emphasis has also been laid on the use of hydrams.

Horticulture:

In the hill areas of Assam and Manipur attempts have been made to introduce horticulture extensively on the field normally given to shifting cultivation. Under the scheme, pineapple, orange and banana are being grown in many places. Apple cultivation proved to be successful in some areas of Arunachal particularly in Kameng district according to a survey by Agro-Economic Research Centre for Northeast India, Jorhat (Gohain, 1977). Problems of transport and marketing have however, appeared as the main hurdle in the growth of horticulture.

Taungiya:

Another approach to the question of limiting the harmful effects of shifting cultivation is Taungiya. This is a combination of sylviculture and impermanent agriculture. Under the system, the cultivators are permitted to clean and burn a part of the forest area and then plant rows of commercially valuable trees. Also, the farmer is permitted to cultivate his own crops between the rows of the new plantations. Within the span of three or four years, the new plantations get well established, when the cultivator is permitted to move to another part in the forest and repeat the process there. Thus the commercially useful varieties of plants are also planted while the cultivator is not made to shed shifting cultivation practice at once. In fact the National Forest Policy Resolution of 1952 emphasized the need of introducing taungiya system to overcome the problem of shifting cultivation.

Some of the state governments and the governments of the union territories have taken many other measures to eliminate the evils of shifting cultivation. Recently under the inspiration of Arunachal Administration the Bangni of Kameng and Papu valleys have started switching over to wet cultivation. A good impact of the demonstration of using plough technique by the State government is reflected in their mode of agriculture.

In recent years in Nagaland the extension agencies have taken steps to encourage scientific jhuming by advising the tribals to make furrows across the slope rather than along it, and also to adopt leguminous and other crops with quick soil regenerating and soil binding capacities. Moreover, shifting cultivation beyond certain degrees of slope has been prohibited in many states.

In Tripura, until recently the forests were not properly demarcated and there was very little restriction on shifting cultivation. The tribal jhumia were allowed to practise shifting cultivation in protected and reserved forest and also in the forest proposed to be reserved. Grazing was also allowed for bona fide use without any fee except in reserved forests and those proposed to be reserved. There was no traditional right of inhabitancy of the forest but the tribals could have forest produce free of royalty. However, in course of time the problem has drawn the attention of the government of Tripura and subsequently steps have been taken to deal with the economic problems related to shifting cultivation. Economic problems of the Jhumia are mainly created due to the 'Dadan' system. Of late, the government has adopted certain measures to check the exhorbitant rates of interest charged on advances supplied to the Jhumias by the Mahajans and has been directly giving loans to the Jhumias at the low rate of only 4 per cent interest per annum. The loan is given when the jhum work is on and is recovered soon after the harvest is over. This measure, however, has not been very successful.

In order to alienate the transition from shifting cultivation to agriculture, it is necessary to examine the techno-economic changes and their concomitant socio-cultural changes and problems at three levels–changes in the hill village, changes in the valley village settled for generation and changes introduced or induced in the government sponsored agricultural colonies.

The government of Orissa since the merger of exstates has tried in all manners to stop shifting cultivation. It brought a large area under reserved forests and settled the shifting cultivator Pauri Bhuiya and other neighbouring tribes, Bentkar, Cherenga (known also as Erenga) Kulha and the Juang in Keonjhar in Jungle clearings, in the valleys and plateaus.

The government of Orissa has also taken up the programme of rotational land use on a watershed basis through the soil conservation department. The programme has the following main aspects:

i) Providing land to the tribal who is willing to give up cultivation on steep slopes.

ii) Plantation of economic species useful for the tribal community.

iii) Introduction of conservation farming to allow tribal people to obtain higher production from crop land.

iv) Utilization of steep slopes for production of timber.

Under this scheme a suitable watershed in the shifting cultivation area is selected and a rotational land use programme is executed on the existing catchment. A schematic land classification of watershed management united together with a land use programme as recommended for watershed areas for rationalization of shifting cultivation has been prepared.

The above programme was initially started in selected catchments of Koraput district on a pilot scale and then it extended to the area of Phulbani, Kalahandi and Keonjhar districts. However, it is felt that these programmes are inadequate in view of the vast population at the area affected by shifting cultivation.

In Madhya Pradesh shifting cultivation was prohibited by law as far back as 1867. Bewar is not permitted anywhere in the state except Baigachack and in some areas of Chhattisgarh. The tribal welfare department of Madhya Pradesh is reported to have rehabilitated a number of Korwa shifting cultivator families in Sarguja.

They are inclined to take up settled agriculture as they have been provided houses and have ceased to be a wandering tribe (Mathur, 1963: 106). Experience has shown that they can continue settled agriculture only if sufficient land is given to support the families as has been done by the government in some cases.

The Forest Control Policy of the Government of Madhya Pradesh has brought with it some remedies and some problems for the Baiga of Central Madhya Pradesh. With the introduction of a money and exchange system, their self sufficiency in food has virtually come to an end and they have become more vulnerable to exploitation by money lenders. The introduction of a contract system has reduced the tribal Baiga to the position of hired labourers. However, the positive aspects of the Forest Control policy should never be overlooked. Introduction of transport and roads in their areas has brought them into direct contact with the outside world. Cultivation of commercial crops and a direct contact with the market is turning them into farmers-cum-traders. They are also gradually adopting plough farming. Contact with the outside world has brought an apparent change in their socio-cultural life which is reflected in their dress, diet, utensils, decoration and festivals.

In Karnataka, till 1902, the tribals were free to practise shifting cultivation. From that year onwards shifting cultivation called *kumri* came under some control. As claimed by the Forest Department of Karnataka notable success has been achieved in turning the Kuruba shifting cultivators into settled cultivators over the past 15 years and they have also been made to adopt large scale plantations. With this perspective they have been allotted old *kumri* lands, devoid of valuable species on the understanding that they are to plant Teak in the areas operated upon. The scheme has been successful to a notable extent and has brought good amounts of money to the Kuruba.

Stricter enforcement of forest regulations has adversely affected the shifting cultivation by the Soliga living in the forest regions. However, no effective and alternative scheme has been adopted for their settlements in their own natural environment, stoppage of, or discontinuing 'Podu' cultivation. Although there are certain restrictions, the Soliga are found to practise 'Podu' cultivation with or without the formal approval of the competent authorities.

A review of the measures undertaken by various state governments in the direction of control on shifting cultivation shows that the measures have certain inherent weaknesses which tend to slow down their implementation. For instance, in case of Orissa, there is a clear contradiction in the steps taken by the two departments of the state government. Whereas the Forest Department tries to enforce a ban on shifting cultivation to protect the forests and forest wealth, the Tribal and Rural Welfare Department would like to improve the shifting cultivation practices maintaining its aim of serving the interest of scheduled tribes. Furthermore, the step taken by various state governments have so far been able to divert only a small proportion of the cultivators engaged in shifting cultivation and hence a greater part of this population still continues to depend upon it. The Dhebar commission concluded "the total replacement of this system, if it comes at all will be a long term process" (Report, 1961: 147).

The present position

There is a continuing controversy over swidden cultivation. According to one view, it is the only practical approach to certain inherent difficulties in preparing a proper seedbed on steep slopes where any disturbance of the surface by hoeing or ploughing will lead to washing away of the fertile top soil. Hence shifting cultivators do not plough or disturb the soil before sowing (Bhowmick, 1977:8). This view could be tenable only if the fallowing period is adequate and consonant to the topography of the area. But it does not appear to be possible due to growing population pressure, depleting carrying capacity of land and scarcity of forested land suitable for jhuming.

The other view regards shifting cultivation as particularly destructive mode of agriculture as it dries up the hill springs, leads to soil erosion and deforestation and thus deprives the people of the benefits of the forest produce. The fertile topsoil which is washed away down to the valley causes sedimentation of the river beds and brings floods in the plain. Thus shifting cultivation affects the life of even the people living in the adjoining valleys.

There are a number of reasons for lowering the yield. Due to shortening of jhum cycle plants do not get sufficient time to grow and at the time of firing for the next clearance the quantity of ash produced is not enough to produce a good yield. Furthermore, due to the thin cover of vegetation and the steeply sloping land the soil becomes porous and thus loses the capacity to retain rain-water resulting in lower yielding crops.

It may be mentioned here that the jhum cycle in different areas has been shortened alarmingly due to shortage of land. This is quite obvious in the Garo Hills of Meghalaya where the jhum cycle has come down from 30-40 years to 10 years or even less (Goswami, 1968: 5-6). Consistent decrease in the carrying capacity of land is also noticeable. The carrying capacity of land under shifting cultivation in the hilly region of N.E. India on an average is estimated to be four to six persons while the density of population in the rural area of Meghalaya is 39 persons per sq km (Borah and Goswami, 1977: 42). In Assam this density is 25 persons per sq km (Saha, 1970:220). This clearly shows that shifting cultivation can hardly provide subsistence to the people.

The land brought under terracing under the subsidy scheme has not been regularly utilized. Due to rapid weed growth and loss of fertility, terrace cultivation in such land was abandoned. Garo cultivators are not conversant with the system of terrace cultivation. It is reported that the abandoned terrace land in Garo hills were later converted into swidden systems (Borah and Goswami, 1977; 46). It has also been observed that the jhum lands being converted to terrace or wet plot are largely unirrigated. The farmers have to depend on rainfall for the terrace or wet cultivation on such land.

The shifting cultivators are unaware of the use of modern tools and chemicals. It has been observed that even those practising terrace cultivation do not have pesticides or chemicals to protect their crops. Besides this there is partial damage of crops by stray cattle and wild birds and animals.

Shifting cultivation is associated with many magico-religious rites and some anthropologists have expressed fear of social disintegration and psychological breakdown among the tribes if any abrupt change is introduced in their agricultural technique without simultaneous change in their magico-religious beliefs. It has been observed through some field studies that in Assam hills magico-religious beliefs of the neighbouring Hindus have left their obvious impact on the hill cultivators. The Garo have started adopting plough cultivation along with the regilious beliefs and rites of the neighbouring Hindus (Das, 1960). The Hajong of the Garo Hills, Lalung of the Mikir Hills and the Jaintia of Jiantia Hills are much influenced by Hinduism as they are adopting plough cultivation.

Due to increasing pressure of their growing population on land the Purum are moving towards permanent plough cultivation in the plains. By cultivating the surplus land of the Meitheis over a period of time the Purum have generated a good surplus of produce and by selling that they have been able to purchase pieces of land for plough cultivation.

Though the jhuming is rejected in many quarters, it contributes considerably to the total agriculture of Tripura. Jhum provides about ten per cent of the total production of rice in the state (Ganguly, 1968,: 52). Vegetables grown in the jhums (mainly gourd and brinjal) come to the market and thus augument the total supply in the plains.

Of late, some of the shifting cultivator jhumias have started earning an income by working as wage labourers in development work undertaken by the government like road construction and employment in government service. Some jhum villages have good communication facilities and are resorting to settled cultivation, horitculture, animal husbandry and poultry. Jhuming in such villages is losing its importance as a major source of income. However, in other villages it is still the most important source of income (Sain, 1978: 11). As a consequence to the developmental work and urban growth, the Lushai Hills on the northern side of the district has come more under urban influence. Even in the subdivision of Lungleh, which is the southern part of the district, near the town or near good communication lines villagers are poor in agriculture in general, and their occupation is diversified. The more we proceed towards the Arakan Hills or further south the more we find villages rich in agriculture and people completely dependent on shifting cultivation, as no other work is available.

In the Keorjhar Hills, where the high population density has forced the people to be satisfied with a small amount of land, villages are very small. With the increase of population, people have been adopting permanent wet cultivation and naturally those who have adopted this system, have temporarily overcome the pressure. On the contrary, those who have not adopted wet cultivation or have no immediate scope of modernization, still continue to practice shifting cultivation. There is diversity of economy among villages in the Keonjhar Hills.

The cropping patterns in the hills have not changed significantly over time and the introduction of new technology of agricultural production has not made much of a dent. The hills enjoy a comparative advantage in the production of plantation crops, off season vegetables and flowers and fruits. (Shah, 1979: 19). But due to various technical, economic institutional and social constraints the potential has not yet been realized.

Some of the reasons for the persistence of shifting cultivation are as follows:

i) The plots of land available for wet cultivation in many cases are small and scattered.

ii) There is a fear of the crop being destroyed by wild animals in scattered plots of land.

iii) Extension programmes are weak. Though most of the agricultural operations in the hills are done by women there are no women extension workers to educate the women agricultural workers in jhum.

iv) Due to lack of ownership of land the Jhumia are not able to get productive credit.

v) Marketing and storage are the biggest bottlenecks in hill farming as farmers do not get adequate returns on their investments.

vi) There is still the dominance of social and religious values and beliefs, such as ideas of hurting the mother earth's breast and this has strengthened the existence of shifting cultivation.

Due to inadequate means of transport and communications most of the tribals are cut off from the mainstream of regional economy. The shifting cultivators hardly have any inclination to produce a surplus in settled or wet cultivation as there is no marketing facility in the hill areas. Due to a complete absence of irrigation facilities or due to inadequate irrigation facilities they can neither use fertilizers nor switch over to wet or settled cultivation. Communal ownership of land is maintained due to the limited number of working hands because of the low density of population. Due to non-fixity of tenurial rights the long term improvement of land has not been encouraged. The provision for co-operative credit is not adequate. If the shifting cultivators do not borrow they have little to invest and if they borrow from money lenders it deprives them of a large part of their produce which they have to return in kind.

The deciding factors in the tribal society are sometimes supernatural rather than human. Per acre return is very small as only low valued crops are cultivated.

In the field study in Meghalaya it was found that the shifting cultivators paid more attention to jhum by devoting a greater part of manpower available and skill and only taking a half-hearted approach to terrace cultivation. A few farmers undertook terrace cultivation just to keep possession of land allotted to them. The potentiality created in the terraced field was found to have remained under utilized. Because of such factors, contrary to the expectation, the yield rate in terrace cultivation was much lower. (Saikia and Kalita, 1979: 92). This tends to confirm that shifting cultivation has deeper roots in the socio-economic life of the concerned tribes, hence a consistent effort is needed to educate them about the gains of the alternative modes. This process must be supplemented by demonstration.

In the study of the selected area of Tripura, Assam, Meghalaya, Mizoram and Arunachal Pradesh by the Agro Economic Research Centre for Northeastern India, it has been observed that shifting cultivation offers very little scope for economic upliftment on account of its subsistence nature. Extension of area is also not possible as this form of agriculture is mainly dependent upon human labour. There is little scope for specialization as diverse crops are shown in a single plot of land. Even when there is some surplus income in some families, the scope for investment for higher production in shifting cultivation is limited. Because of the land being communally owned the individual farmer does not take interest in the land development. Shifting cultivation has been continuing because there is no alternative in most of the hill villages (Saikia and Kalita, 1979: 112).

However, the technique developed by expert agriculturists such as Apa-Tanis and Angami Naga is ideally suited to local conditions and can serve as a model for the dvelopment of agriculture among less advanced tribes of the neighbourhood. The introduction of terrace cultivation among the shifting cultivator Sema Nagas with the help of Angami instructors has greatly relieved the pressure on the land in over-populated Sema country. Similarly the agricultural method of the Apa-Tanis has to some extent been initated by the neighbouring Dafla and could, if adapted to local conditions, result in a considerable increase of food production among other tribes of the Subansiri area.

The major reasons for the existence of shifting cultivation among the Maler is the geographical setting of the villages. However, for a pretty long time the process of change from khallu land to Bari land, from shifting cultivation to settled and plough cultivation has been known to the Maler. In all the possibilities they have responded positively to such changes. On their own initiative the percentage of Bagri land has increased. This has been the observation of Vidyarthi in his field work (Vidyarthi, 1975: 323).

The Soliga have preference for shifting cultivation. Even those who have been given lands for settled cultivation have been seen to go in for the shifting cultivation keeping their land fallow. But those who came in contact with peasants of the plains village have taken to settled agriculture as in the case of Purani and Guruvinagadde settlements (Morab, 1977: 17).

The kolams who shifted to Manikgarh forest in Rajura Talug of Andhra Pradesh were found to be reluctant to take to plough cultivation and preferred to stick to *podu.* Even where Kolams have completed the transition to permanent cultivation their enterprise has hardly found the expected encouragement either from the administration or the neighbouring population.

The socio-economic conditions of tribal groups in different areas differ considerably and hence no blanket scheme can be successful in weaning the shifting cultivators away from it. Some of the programmes undertaken to introduce settled farming have not given the desired results. This is mainly because of the fact that land capability classification of hilly areas is not done as yet. High yield varieties of crops and improved implements suitable for different attitudes of the hilly areas are yet to be developed.

No single remedy to deal with the problems for the entire tribal region is conceivable. Depending upon the agro-climatic conditions, a mix of activities, such as terracing, orchard plantations, forestry and forest based industries will have to be introduced. Furthermore, some extent of jhum cultivation may have to continue not only because of emotional and socio-cultural factors but because it seems to represent the best economic opportunity in certain relatively remote and sparsely populated pockets. Nagaland, Arunachal Pradesh and Mizoram could be cases in point.

Chapter Six

SUMMARY AND CONCLUSIONS

The review reveals that swidden cultivation in the areas where it is practised is largely a matter of natural resource management. The ecology is such that no other system of cultivation can be resorted to. In the Amarpur Block of Tripura it is seen that some of the Reang tribals have both kinds of land, the hill slopes as well as the wet valley lands. It seems that they acquired the level wet lands later. They practice swidden cultivation on the slopes but have leased the wet lands to the immigrants from Bangladesh. They do not perceive swidden as a more primitive agricultural technique than settled cultivation. They have themselves not taken to plough cultivation as they have been used to swidden which keeps them busy all the year round. Thus swidden represents the community's adjustment to the ecosystem in which they have been placed. In the course of time the socio-cultural system meshes up with the agro-eco system and a stage is reached when the former revolves round the latter to such an extent that cultural myths which militate against any alternative system are created. These now serve as barriers against the adoption of settled cultivation.

Since swidden is a subsystem of the bigger agro-eco system, the changes in the latter must impinge on the former. Anthropological studies in the past have highlighted the traditional ethnographic dimension and the cultural barriers which have set the people against it. They have paid little attention to the changes in the traditional way of life as result of external factors. This process has been accelerated in recent years. The rapid economic development after independence, the growing demand for land as a factor of production, the increasing demand and the prices of timber have imposed constraints on the availability of land for traditional swidden cultivators. The problem has been further aggravated by rapid population growth much beyond the carrying capacity of land in such areas. In addition to these factors there was growing exposure to ideas and new technology from outside. This was possible through opening up of the tribal areas through development of new means of communication as well as the spread of education. Growth of political consciousness has also taken place on account of mobilization by political parties on the eve of every general election. Demands for new facilities and ways for attaining a higher standard of living are being articulated. The government is also committed to such a course. Efforts are being made through enormous financial inputs to raise their income beyond the subsistence level. The state policy towards swidden cultivation may be viewed in this perspective.

It has been pointed out that the cultural imperatives in swidden communities are so strong that they are averse to any change from shifting to settled cultivation. As a matter of fact there are socio-cultural constraints in any process of change in all communities. This does not mean that change is not taking place in those communities or that attempts to that end should not be made. Even if we accept cultural determinism, change does take place under the pressure of diverse factors over a period of time. And even before this happens some innovation-prone individuals even in traditional cultures begin to experiment with new ideas and artifacts. This produces demonstration effect on others. Human individuals are rational thinking entities and not mere automatons controlled by culture.

This is seen in many areas in which social scientists discounted any possibility of change due to strong social taboos against settled cultivation. The Baiga in many areas, the Garo and several tribes of Assam have been taking to settled cultivation. Vidyarthi (1963) also points out that the Maler of Rajmahal Hills have also been moving towards settled cultivation in such areas where this is possible. During the Second Plan period the relocation scheme for some shifting cultivators did not succeed; not so much on account of the cultural factors but on account of faulty administrative arrangements, putting people in a hostile social set up and lack of adequate preparation for the change. The administrators were happy that their failures were hidden under the cover of the tribal's opposition to change per se.

While weaning communities from shifting cultivation would be a slow process, it is realised that at no point of time would it be possible to relocate the entire population engaged in this on level ground. The pressure of population on the plains is so intense that it is difficult to find it for settling even such tribals who are willing to do so. The other strategy should therefore be to promote scientific swidden cultivation. Thus minimal damage would be done to the subsoil, erosion would be checked and a better tilling-fallow ratio can be maintained. Along with this, efforts should be made to build terraces wherever possible. This is a difficult and expensive process but tribals in many areas have proved equal to this task. With enhanced financial support from the government this process might be accelerated.

An effort can be made to encourage the cultivation of perennial and other cash crops. This will not only raise their income level but will make them sedentary wherever they are. The carrying capacity of the land would increase substantially and the swidden cultivators would be brought closer to the regional and national economy. This step will also further the process of national integration.

In order to supplement the income of swidden cultivators, animal husbandry programmes should be worked out effectively. Since grazing is easily available, better breeds of cattle, goats and pigs should be introduced in the area. From the sale of these animal products the people would make some money and even if they are not able to sell, at least their own food resources will be augmented and they would be able to ward off starvation which faces them in certain parts of the year,

On account of ignorance of the actual conditions and also of the powerless position of the shifting cultivators, the government and people at large have tended to regard shifting cultivation as an environmental and socio-cultural problem. In most areas the function of the governments has been regulatory. Time has come to take a holistic view of the problem. Shifting cultivation is a response to demands of an eco-system, it is an adjustment with a given environment, Any effort to deal with it effectively should be multi-pronged and based on a detailed survey of each area. Research should be multi-disciplinary in character. It should include both human and natural resource aspects to attain an optimum quality of life and environmental quality through the formulation of an optimum set of decisions.

Chapter One

INDIA

A Case Study

The Research Site

Although, swidden cultivation is practised in many isolated pockets both in Middle and South India, I chose to work in the East Indian province of Arunachal Pradesh as it is the traditional home of swiddeners; the bulk of its people eke out their existence through this method of cultivation. This is also an area in which change is taking place at a lightning speed. Government policies have produced results sometimes beyond the expectations of the administration. The sensitiveness of the administration to people's sentiments in this area is much higher than in other parts of the country. In this land, awakened to new expectations, I chose one of the most primitive tribes, the Wancho, who are located high up on the hills at the tri-junction of Burma, Arunachal Pradesh and Nagaland.

The Locale

On the North-East border of India lies the sprawling territory of Arunachal Pradesh. On the west, it skirts Bhutan and on the north lies the Tibet region of the Republic of China. On the east, it has common frontier with Burma. It is the home of a large number of tribes. The total population in 1981 was 628,050. Tirap district which lies on the extreme south of Arunachal Pradesh is the home of the Wancho tribe. This district has highest density of population in Arunachal Pradesh. It holds 14 persons to a square kilometre. The population is entirely rural.

The Wancho live in the Longding sub-division in the extreme south-western part of the district. The entire area is rugged and

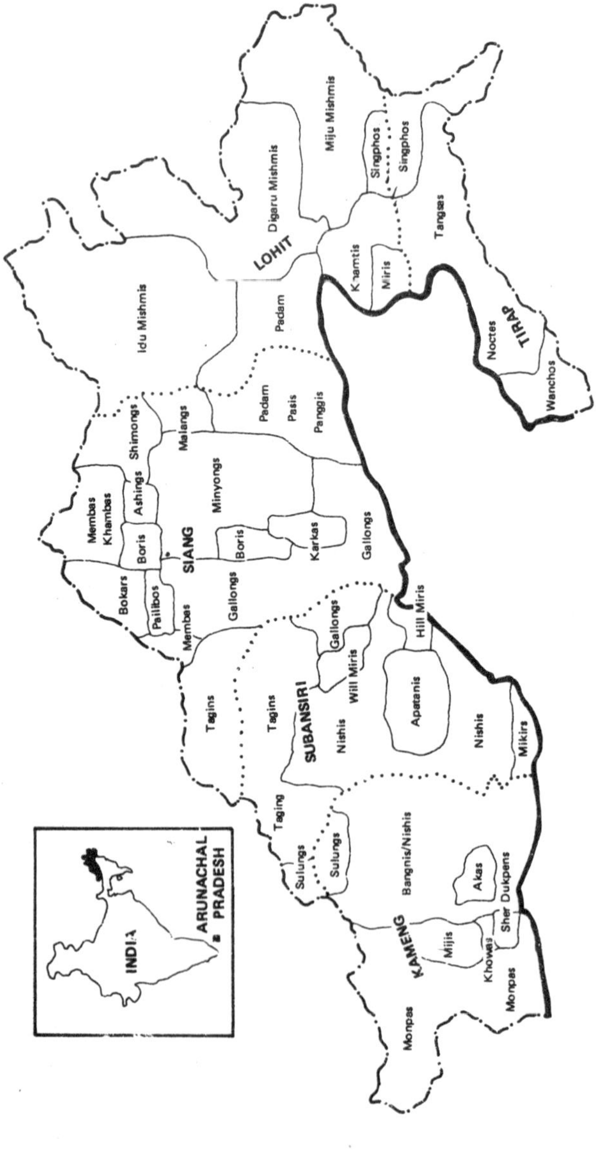

ARUNACHAL PRADESH
DISTRIBUTION OF TRIBAL GROUPS

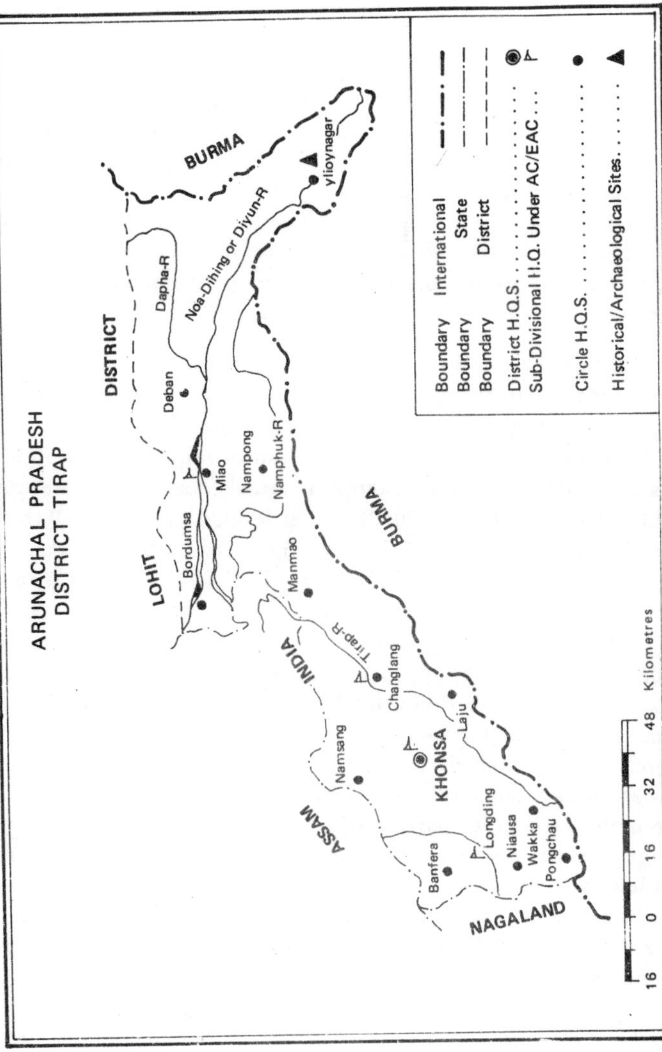

Based upon Survey of India Map with the Permission of the Surveyor General of India.

mountainous. It is dominated by the Patkoi mountain which separates the district from Burma. The mountain descends into the plains in the West through a series of hills. The vegetation on the whole is tropical evergreen rain forest type and semi-evergreen depending upon the altitude and soil condition. There are very few grasslands and these are located in the comparatively less humid areas. The most important river in this area is Tissa. There are some shallow lakes in this area formed by the old beds of the meandering rivers. These lakes have now become natural fisheries. Besides the rivers, the springs are the main sources of water supply in the village settlements.

The flora of the district are rich in variety. The vegetation of the area consists largely of tropical and subtropical ever-green forests interspersed with the grasslands and temperate forests in the high hills. Due to the age-old practice of swiddening only secondary forests are found. A forest canopy is usually formed by spreading branches of the tall trees. On the lower level, we find less tall trees. In the slightly open areas clumps of fan-leafed palm and fishtailed palm are occasionally seen. Large clumps of giant bamboos are also there. The trees are entwined by large woody climbers and creepers often connecting adjoining trees and forming festoons of branches hanging loosely from the top. Among these climbers is the climbing palm and cane. These canes are largely used by the local people. Besides cane, wild pepper is also found along with aroids and orchids. The orchids are extremely beautiful. On lower heights, a number of shrubs are found, some of them with the flowers and some without. In the moist dark spots, particularly where humus is present, there is dense growth of mushrooms. There is also a large variety of ferns which lend additional charm to the greenery. Along the openings of the forests besides the streams, there is large gregarious growth of banana. These wild bananas offer good material for breeding and improving the cultivated banana. In the occasional placid pools, lotus is also seen. In the grassland, we find a number of yellow and pink mauve flowers which look extremely pretty in the vast green spans. The flora in these parts are of considerable interest since they represent a meeting point for the Eastern Asia and Burma-Malayan floristic elements.

The fauna of the area, like the flora, are equally rich and varied. There are some rare specimen of wild animals and birds

The area is frequented by some paleoarctic species and migratory species of birds that breed in north of the Himalayas. The birds of Indian sub-region are also well represented. Water fowls and ducks are commonly found in the river water and the pools. Parakeets, broad-bills, the mountain thrush, the golden backed wood-pecker and hill myna are commonly met with. On the hill slopes, the bulbul, spotted dove, quails, horn bills, partridges and the pigeons are met with.

Among the carnivorous mammals we find the tiger and leopard. Big cats are also found in the forest. Elephants are common in areas covered by bamboos and sal trees. The Samkhar and deer prefer to live near human settlements. The Indian bison, wild buffaloes, mithun *(bos frontaris)* and wild boar live in the grassy and bushy jungles. The Chinese Pangolin is also found in this area. Various types of rats and squirrel are found near villages. In the rivers and ponds, a large variety of fish is found. It forms an important item in the diet of the tribals.

The elevation of the land varies from 200 metres in the north-west to 4,000 metres over the mountains. There are peaks which rise to 4,500 metres. The climatic conditions vary from place to place due to the mountainous nature of the terrain. The climate is cool and highly humid at lower elevation and in the valleys. The cold season starts from November. From March to May, there are frequent thunder-storms and pre-monsoon showers. On the whole, the climate in the hill areas is moderate and pleasant and the constant breeze makes it salubrious. The annual rainfall ranges between 250-400 cms. increasing from north-west to south-east. The rain, however, decreases above the height of 1,500 metres. The bulk of the rain is received from June through October. January is the coldest month. The minimum temperature in the plains is 12°c. On the hills, however, temperature in winter goes below 0°c at an elevation of 3,000 metres and above.

Profile of the Study Villages

The study has been conducted among the Wancho in the Tirap district of Arunachal Pradesh. For the purpose of the study, five villages – Pongchaw, Niausa, Rusa, Mintong and Zedua – have been selected the inhabitants of which are practising swidden cultivation as the main and only method of agriculture. Though in recent years wet rice cultivation has also been introduced in some of the villages close to the plains border of Assam yet the entire Wancho area is practising the swidden method of cultivation. For this study, people have been interviewed through interview schedules about their perception of swidden cultivation and the problems connected with it.

1. Pongchaw

Pongchaw village is situated at 71.2° east latitude and 46.9° south longitude and 4,680 ft. (1,560 mtrs.) above sea level. The east and north side of this village is surrounded by the Tissa river. To the west is Bonia village and to the south lies the territory of Nagaland.

This village is situated just near the Pongchaw Circle headquarters. The Circle Officer is the administrative head of the area. Pongchaw is under Pongchaw-Wakka Community Development (C.D.) Block established in the year 1978-1979. The Pongchaw Circle consists of nine villages. Pongchaw covers a large geographical area of about 6 sq. km. The total population of this village is 1,533 distributed among 184 families. The average family size is 8.33. Pongchaw is the terminus of the road Khonsa. It is a motorable all weather road and the Pongchaw *Anchal Samiti* bus plies over there on alternate days. There is one inter village school situated at Pongchaw headquarters. Students from Pongchaw and nearby villages go to this school for their education. Government has provided hostel and other facilities including board and clothing to the students coming from Pongchaw and other villages. Moreover, Pongchaw also has an Adult Education Centre which is located in the Pongchaw I.V. School. Adult literacy classes are held every evening. To provide the medical facilities to the villagers Government has established a hospital with a Medical Officer and a Compounder in Pongchaw C.O. headquarters. People of Pongchaw Circle depend primarily upon this hospital.

2. Mintong

Mintong is located in the Longding Circle. It is about 18 **km.** from Longding. The village is situated at an altitude of about 4,400 ft. above sea level. To the east of this village is Wakka Circle, to the west of it lies Pamao. To the north there is Niausa village and to the south there is Longphong village. The immediate administrative, judicial and other responsibilities rest with the Extra Assistant Commissioner (EAC) who is stationed at Longding. The total population of Mintong village is 1,019 distributed among 145 families (average family size 7.02). Mintong is situated just near the Khonsa-Pongchaw main road. A jeepable road connects it to the main road. Movement of the people depends only upon the *Anchal Samiti* bus plying between Pongchaw and Khonsa. The village has one Lower Primary School. Government has introduced some development projects in the Wancho area for economic development. In Mintong village the Forest Department has demonstrated the plantation of tea, coffee, big cardamom, bamboo etc. so that the tribal people can be diverted from swidden cultivation. This will help develop their economy.

3. Niausa

Niausa is located in the Longding Circle and situated at a distance of 12 km. south west of Longding. This village is situated at an altitude of about 4,200 ft. above sea level. To the east of this village there is Wakka Circle, to the west there is Pornmo, to the north there is Nianu village and to the south there is Mintong village. The immediate administrative, judicial and other responsibilities rest with the Extra Assistant Commissioner based in Longding. The total population of Niausa village is 1,088 distributed among 150 families (average family size 7.25). Niausa village is situated near the Pongchaw-Khonsa road and at a height of about 150 ft. from the road level. There is no road connecting the village with the main road. The *Anchal Samiti* bus plies over Pongchaw-Khonsa road on alternate days. The Niausa Inter Village School is situated just near the main road. Students from Niausa and nearby villages go for their education to this school. There is a hostel where students get fooding and clothing. Moreover, the Vivekanand Kendriya Vidyalaya is also situated near Niausa village just opposite to the Niausa School. These two institutions provide educational facilities to the village children.

4. Zedua

Zedua is also located in the Longding Circle at a distance of about 2 km. west of EAC headquarters. This village is situated at an altitude of about 4,177.33 ft. above sea level. To the east of the village there is Longding, to the west there lies the territory of Nagaland, to the north is Tissing river and to the south is Chating village. The total population of Zeuda village is 520 distributed among 69 families (average family size 7.53). There is Lower Primary School in Zedua village with total enrolment of about 37 pupils. Free education and other facilities have been provided by the government. Very recently the government introduced midday meals for the students. Moreover, the higher secondary school, situated at a distance of about 2 km. from this village at Longding, provides higher education to other children of the village. There is a jeepable road connecting this village with Longding. There is regular bus service to other places from Longding. The Arunachal State Transport bus plies regularly between Khonsa and Longding. This is the only means of communication.

5. Rusa

Rusa covers a large geographical area of about 5 sq. km. This village is situated at a distance of about 38 km. from Longding. This village comes under Kanubari Circle and the administrative and judicial responsibilities are with the Circle Officer Kanubari. Rusa village is situated on the foothills and it is very close to the Assam border. The total population of Rusa village is 771, distributed among 130 families (average family size 5.93). There is one school in Rusa village with three teachers. For higher studies students have to go outside the village. The communication system of Rusa village is bad. There is a jeepable road connecting this village with Longding. There is also another jeepable road connecting this village with the plains of Assam via Bimalapur. People of this village have close contact with the plains of Assam. People go there to sell their agricultural produce and to buy their day-to-day needs like salt, cloth, coloured beads, gun powder etc. from the markets of Bimalapur, Sapekhati and Borhat.

Ethnographic Background

The Wancho are akin to Konyak Naga and have similar myth of origin and migration. Earlier the tribe was known under the blanket name of eastern Naga. The present name Wancho became popular only after the administration of the area was taken over by the Indian government after Independence in 1947. The Wancho have been occupying the territory for many centuries. The Wancho villages on the foothills had contact with the plains people of Assam. These relations were generally friendly. During the Ahom and the British period, there were frequent inter-village raids and feuds among the Wancho. After Independence, however, the situation has changed and the people have been brought into closer contact with the administration.

According to the 1971 census the numerical strength of the Wancho is 28,642. The sex ratio is 965 females per thousand males. The Wancho live in 41 villages scattered over an area of about 2,302 sq. kms. covering the foothills as well as the habitations located at about 5,000 ft. The density of population is about 12 persons per sq. km.

Social Stratification

Wancho society is rigidly stratified into four main classes. The highest of these is the *Wangham* class which includes the chiefs, who enjoy all the privileges and receive highest social esteem. They are pivots around whom all life and activities in the village revolve. The lowest class is composed of the *Wangpan* who are the commoners. Between these two classes there are two other classes, namely, the *Wanghsa* and *Wanghsus,* whose members have sprung from inter-class marriages. The Wanghsa are the descendents of Wangham fathers and Wangpan mothers (hypergamous unions), whereas the Wanghsus are said to have descended from marriages between Wangpan men and Wangham women (hypogamous unions). In the social hierarchy, the Wanghsa occupy the second position and the Wanghsus the third. The social position of the classes is fixed. The offsprings of parents belonging to the chief's family would continue to be Wangham. The social distinction does not become obvious in the ordinary course of life. It comes to light during social functions when the entire community participates. On such occasions, Wangpan who are at the bottom of the hierarchy are not allowed to take meals sitting in the same row as the Wangham. The Wangpan can never aspire to marry a girl who is above him in status but a Wangham can easily take a Wangpan girl for his wife. The top three classes practically control the society and the Wangpan execute the decisions of these classes.

Family and Marriage

The smallest unit of the Wancho society is the nuclear family consisting of father, mother and their children. They also follow the joint family system. The grown up boys of the village sleep apart in bachelor's dormitories called *morungs*. There is no separate dormitory for unmarried girls. But they also do not spend the night in their own houses. They sleep in the house of some widow who is distantly related to them. When a family becomes too large and it is difficult to accommodate all the members in a house, the married younger sons establish separate houses for their families. The eldest son stays in the ancestral house and continues to look after his old parents. Married girls leave their parents' house when they are pregnant. Wancho custom does not permit delivery of the first child at the wife's parents' house. In the joint family, all the members take their meals from a common hearth. The management of the kitchen and the cooking of food are the responsibilities of the eldest female member of the family, who is either the wife of the head of the family or the eldest son's wife. All the immates work together for the common interest of the family.

All movable and immovable properties, such as cultivable lands, bamboo groves and kitchen gardens, livestock, granary, utensils, ornaments and guns are held in common by the family. The father is the sole owner of the property which is inherited by the eldest son after his death. Women have no claim over the family property except for the articles given to a daughter in her marriage. Besides the family property, individuals have some personal possessions which are given as gravegoods on their death. No property held by the family is allowed to be sold or distributed without the permission of the head of the family. The Wancho follow the rule of primogeniture in the male line. The family property is not distributed when it breaks up, with other sons establishing their own households. The eldest son who inherits the property may, however, donate homestead plots to his brothers, but they do not have any legal claim on the family property. The family norms demand that all other members of the parental family render help to the newly established family unit. Daughters have no claim whatsoever on the property. A daughter is entitled only to ornaments, clothing, one basket, one scraper, one iron stick, one *dao* and a raincoat which are given at the time of her marriage. She cannot even lay any claim to the property of her husband.

Both monogamy and polygyny are socially and legally recognised by the society. Monogamy is the general rule of marriage, but polygyny is in vogue among the chiefs. A commoner may take a second wife only when the first one is barren or suffers from some incurable disease or is regarded as a liability in the family for some reason or other. Plurality of wives enhances one's social status. Polyandry is unknown. A cross cousin is regarded as a potential spouse.

Clan exogamy is the fundamental rule of marriage among the Wancho. If anybody violates this rule, he will not only be excommunicated but may even be exterminated.

Wancho society is very much class conscious and marriage is not permitted in normal circumstances between boys and girls of different social strata. The sons and daughters of a chief generally marry in another chief's family. The tribe itself is endogamous and marriages are mostly confined to the same village, except in the case of chiefs, who by custom marry at least one wife from another village.

Free mixing of the girls and boys gives them an opportunity to choose their partners in life. The consent of parents is obtained later. But, generally marriages are arranged by the parents. In all sexual relations, incest is the most dreaded and its horror is deep-rooted in the minds of the young Wanchos. Stray cases of incest are reported, but they are very rare. The rule prohibiting an incestuous marriage applies also to marriage within the clan. Inter-tribal marriages are discouraged.

Cross-cousin marriage is socially recognised and preferred. Marriage by exchange of sisters between two families is also preferred. Sororate and levirate are allowed, but a man cannot marry the sister of his wife during the latter's lifetime. Divorce is permitted on payment of fines.

In the case of a negotiated marriage in the Wancho society, the girl is betrothed at a ceremony called *hawanle* or *toimonmonk.* From that time the girl pays visits to the house of the boy who is socially recognised as her husband and the two can cohabit. However, the girl continues to live with her own parents till she conceives. At this time, she is tattooed on one of her thighs. A feast is arranged on this occasion and all the relatives, friends and villagers are invited. This is called *hutu.* Thereafter the girl is taken to the house of her husband by her relatives and friends. On her arrival in her husband's house, she is again tattooed, this time on the breast. This tattooing is called *Khahutu,* and the occasion is also celebrated with a feast for the relatives and friends. From now on the bride stays with her husband. The couple pays a brief visit to the bride's parents after a week. In cases of levirate, sororate, and of love-marriages or in any other form of marriage no such ceremonies and rituals are performed.

Religion and Rituals

The religious beliefs and practices of the Wancho are inextricably inter-woven with the magical beliefs and practices in their everyday life. On one occasion or the other they take resort to such practices. The Wancho also propitiate a number of spirits by offering sacrifices on different occasions.

The Wanchos make sacrifices and offerings to propitiate *Bau-rang,* the god of earth in order to appease him and to save themselves from his curse and anger. There are a number of rituals observed in connection with sickness, disease and calamity conducted by the diviner or the priest. Some religious festivals called *Sangaam, Pagam* and *Gakgam* are performed annually. On these occasions villagers collect their weapons, guns, spears, *dao* etc. at one place. A big red cock is killed by the priest and its blood is sprinkled on all the weapons. The cock thus sacrificed is taken to the paddy field by a priest called *Gipa,* who recites certain incantations while shaking the sacrificed cock. This ritual is to secure a bumper crop and good fortune to the villagers in hunting and other expeditions. After this, the villagers go for hunting to the nearby forest and if the hunt is successful, they celebrate it with a good feast. The installation of a new Chief involves a ceremony with elaborate rituals.

The various festivals, observed by people throughout the year impart a sense of joy and fraternity amongst the people.

The Wancho have a number of agricultural, social and religious festivals. The names and the number of the festivals vary from village to village and also among the different groups of the Wancho. For example, sixteen different festivals are celebrated in a year at Wakka, whereas in Pumao area, only six festivals are observed. In Pongchau, seven festivals are observed.

One of the most important festivals observed all over the Wancho area is *Ojiyele.* This festival is celebrated with great enthusiasm for six to twelve days during March-April just after sowing of *jhum* (swidden) paddy. Pigs, buffaloes and *mithuns* are sacrificed and feasts are arranged in each and every *morung.* Songs and dances by boys and girls in ceremonial costumes make the occasion joyous and colourful. Farm houses are constructed for new harvest. *Ojiyele* takes a very festive look at Pumao where dances are held around a long ceremonial pole called *jangban* planted for this occasion.

The Wancho also observe many other festivals connected with sowing and harvesting rites. *Sakila* and *Chachai* festivals are held to celebrate the sowing of millet and paddy seeds in the field. Successful harvesting of millets is the occasion of another festival called *Chachaban. Lanudongle, Chachiywan* and *Poatak-le* are also harvest festivals. On the occasion of *Chachiyawan* festival, seeds of millet mixed with a sacrificed hen's blood are sprinkled before the millet is brought home from the field, and at the time of *Poatak-le* a few grains of millet are thrown over the earth by the mistress of the house, apparently for a better crop next time.

Death Rituals

The Wancho believe that death due to old age, or prolonged illness, is natural death willed by God. But premature death or death due to accident or sudden illness is believed to be the evil action of the earth god called *Bau-rang.*

The Wancho do not dispose of a dead body before twenty-four hours or so and they keep it inside the house for mourning. The dead body of a chief is placed in a wooden coffin, but that of a commoner is wrapped by a mat or a cloth. The relatives, family friends and villagers, both men and women, go together to the funeral ground where the dead body is placed on a platform about five to six feet above the ground. A small shed is made over the platform and near it an effigy of wood or bamboo is placed with the personal possessions of the deceased hanging from a pole. Sometimes, the relatives of the deceased keep watch on the dead body for several days. At the time of the disposal of the dead body, an animal is sacrificed for a feast and the family members offer a share of their meal each day in the name of the deceased. Purgatory rites are performed after about a month when the dead body is completely decomposed. The skull, which is detached from the dead body by an old man and washed carefully, is wrapped in a red cloth. It is then placed under stones on an auspicious day. This occasion is celebrated with joy and gaiety throughout the village. Before the ceremony starts, a number of people set out to catch fish. They cook the fish with rice and offer it to the soul of the dead. They also tie a bundle of fish and rice to the skull as offerings to the soul.

The chief's corpse is retained for seven days, the skull is detached on the eighth day. After the skull is removed, it is exposed while the people go on singing and dancing around it. On this occasion, the villagers contribute their mite for a feast. When the feasting and rejoicings are over, the skull is placed in a stone urn. In cases of unnatural death, these rituals are not followed and the corpse is kept exposed in the jungle.

The day when the skull is detached is marked with a ceremony called *rapoley* or *ja foatle*. Thereafter, every year during *paotakle* festival, skulls of all the deceased members of the family are taken out and offerings of rice beer and cooked food are made to them.

Priests and Diviners

Among the Wancho, there are certain gradations of priests and their assignments differ according to rank and position. The *gampa* or *gipa* or *rami* is regarded as the principal priest. Next to him is the *aupa* or *opa*, a village diviner. Then follows the *ngopa*, a household diviner and after him comes the *rampa* who performs the obsequies. The last is the *aje*, a medicine man, who is also capable of falling into a trance. The priests treat the sick with their magical power as well as medicines. A priest is considered to be a person with superior spiritual powers. Among the Wancho, a large number of such religious functionaries are found in the Wakka area.

The profession of a priest or diviner is not hereditary; anyone, whether man or woman, having acquired sufficient knowledge of the procedure and paraphernalia of the craft may aspire to the position. The tradition is handed down orally to successive generations. Though there is no restriction to a woman becoming diviner, provided she has mastered the knowledge, in usual practice, the priesthood is a profession for men, and not women.

Divination

A characteristic feature of the tribal religion is the observance of the divination before embarking on any important task, such as building of houses, sowing in the field, setting out on a long journey, organising a social festival, performing a religious rite, naming of a new-born child etc. The divination for ascertaining success of an expedition is examined by the priest after sacrificing a cock or a chicken or by breaking eggs. Among the Wancho, the divination is observed by breaking eggs; the position of the broken shells of the eggs indicates good or bad fortune.

Houses, Dress and Decorations

The dwelling houses of the people, except the Government buildings, are all bamboo and wooden structures. The houses are strengthened and secured with cane strings. The level for the floor is obtained by driving stilts, wooden or bamboo, into the hillside. An open bamboo platform, generally rectangular in shape extends outwards from the main house on one side in the front. This serves the purpose of a courtyard, which is also used for drying the food-stuff. The walls of the front room, which serves as a common room, are decorated with hunted trophies and heads of *mithuns* and other animals sacrificied on different occasions. The main house is a long hall with small partition walls dividing the rooms. The houses are spacious. The roof is high and slanting, and the interior of the house without windows appears dark.

Generally, houses are built by the local people on co-operative and reciprocal basis. The building materials are collected from the nearby forests by those who want to construct a house, and the labour is supplied freely by the villagers. The owner of the house feeds those who help.

An important structure which plays a vital role in the communal life of the tribal people of this district is the *morung* or village dormitory. There may be a number of *morungs* in a village according to its size and need. The *morung* is a centre of training for the young people as well as a council and guard house. A *morung* is also a sleeping place for the male bachelors. The Noctes and Wanchos have separate sleeping places for boys and girls. The Wancho chiefs have their own special *morung* called *wanghampa* or *panu* which is, in fact, a council house. It was used in the old days as a repository of human heads collected during head-hunting expeditions resulting from tribal feuds. Wancho morungs are also storehouses of antique wood-carvings and of animal heads. Usually, there are separate morungs in a Wancho village for separate village units called *jong*.

The Wancho are averse to the use of full dress. They are scantily clad, but they are fond of body decoration. They love ornamentation and manage to produce a very picturesque effect. The materials chiefly used are shell, ivory, boar's tusk, beads of agate and other pebbles, goat's hair dyed scarlet and in other colours, brass, and glass.

The dress of a Wancho male consists of a loin cloth and a coloured shoulder band. A wrapper is used during the cold season. Women's dress comprises a waist cloth and a shawl. The exposure of the body above the waist by both men and women is common. Wancho men and women are very fond of head-dresses and ornaments. Hair-pins of cane and bone are also used with the head-dress. The Wancho women as well as the chiefs use necklaces of coloured beads. Both men and women wear armlets. Armlets of ivory are used by men and those of lead by women. Earrings, earplugs and belts made of cane, some of which are studded with wool and beads, are used by both men and women.

Tattooing has a very special significance for the Wancho. Besides being personal decoration, it has both social and ritual import. Apart from the rank and social status of a person, different designs of tattooing on different parts of the body signify attainment of different stages in life, particularly in case of women.

A man from the chief's family has very elaborate designs all over the body while others, lower in rank, have simple ones. A head-hunter has special designs on the face and body as marks of bravery.

Food and Cooking

The basic diet of the people consists of cereals, millets, vegetables and meat. But job's tears, millet and maize are more commonly taken, and they are supplemented by sweet potatoes, arum or *kachu.* A very large variety of wild leafy vegetables, roots, tubers and fruits as well as pumpkin, brinjal (egg-plant), ginger, onion, mustard leaves, chilli, the flowers of plantain, mushroom and bamboo shoots are also included in the diet. The people are fond of fish, but there are restrictions on meat. The domestic animals, pigs and chicken are regarded as special items of meal and are eaten on sacrificial occasions. Meat and fish are often dried up and stocked for future consumption, especially during scarcity. The foodstock is kept on the rack built above the hearth in almost every house.

Most food is boiled, though meat is sometimes roasted. Rice and millet are boiled with vegetables to which chillies and salt are added for flavour. They do not, however, use oil or fat. Food grains are pounded into powder and then mixed with hot water for making a paste. The paste is poured into bamboo tubes for baking and later taken with salt, chillies, vegetables, meat or fish. Condiments of bamboo-shoots are also edible.

Local beer is brewed from rice, tapioca and millets. Liquors are prepared by special process of fermentation and distillation. The people also take tea without sugar or milk. They are accustomed to chewing areca nuts with betel.

Dance and Music

The Wancho are fond of music; their songs are rich in melody and rhythm. The life of the people, their love and emotions, find expression in their songs. The compositions are many and varied for different occasions. There are group songs sung on the occasion of pounding rice, harvesting crops, performing the group dance and so on. These apart, the young people sing love-songs in the form of dialogues. It is a pleasure to listen to the tribal nursery rhymes which the children recite while playing. Similarly, their cradle songs sung at a low pitch which melody predominating over rhythm are pleasing.

Festivals, as stated before, are the special occasions for dances. The dance is generally performed in a group. The dancers wearing colourful costumes keep balance and rhythm in harmony with songs and music maintaining the tempo of the dance. Drums and gongs are commonly used as musical instruments. On some occasions boys and girls dance together. Indeed, the hard life in the hills is in a way greatly redeemed by the rapturous, colourful and invigorating communal dances expressing the feelings and emotions of the people.

The war dance of the Wancho performed on the occasion of a victory or a successful head-hunting expedition of the old days is now held to commemorate the old tradition and to keep up the high spirit of the tribe.

The Wancho perform dances on many other occasions, such as a chief's death or construction of a new house. Both boys and girls participate in the dance performed during the *Ojiyele* festival. Songs and beating of log drums accompany some of the dances. Some dances are organised in the *morung.*

The Chief

The chief is the supreme authority in the village. Each village, whether it is the paramount village or its offshoot, has a chief. The origin of chiefship is shrouded in mystery. It is, however, obvious that constant raids and feuds necessitated an office in which authority was centralised for the maintenance of law and order. The office of the chief is hereditary. It is inherited by the eldest son of a chief born of a Wanghsia wife. In the event of the absence of male child by such a wife, the Wangham of an allied village is offered the office of the chief. In the Wancho society great sanctity is attached to this office and the installation of new chief is a big event for the whole village. The chief is the fountain of all honour. He is the dispenser of justice. He is the chief administrator and cannot be deposed. He enjoys a number of prerogatives such as free labour for cultivation of his lands and construction of houses. He enjoys the largest and the best plot in the *Jhum* field. Similarly, he has a lion's share in hunting and fishing. He receives gifts from villagers who also contribute to his granary as a token of respect and in recognition of the power that he wields. The chief has certain obligations to the people. He has to look after their welfare and help them in the time of distress. He is responsible for the safety and well-being of all his villagers. He guides and controls the political life of the village, arbitrates in disputes and decides civil and criminal cases. He is also in-charge of organizing developmental activities. In the olden days he used to lead hunting campaigns. He can inflict punishment on a person found guilty of any offence. In this matter, he consults the village council of elders. He is a symbol of the unity of the village. He is obliged to take advice from the village council. Although the wind of change is visible, the office of the chief still carries great respect and authority. No development effort in the Wancho area can succeed without his active co-operation.

Swidden Operations

The Wancho are swidden cultivators as are many tribals in the hill areas of eastern and central India. It is estimated that in India 929,480 hectares of land is utilised for swidden cultivation on which 2.6 million people subsist. In Arunachal Pradesh the state to which the Wancho belong, out of a total cultivated area of 133,435 hectares, 101,329 hectares are under swiddening; only 24,207 hectares are under wet rice cultivation.

By and large, swidden cultivation is practised in the hilly terrain where the slope of the land, high rainfall, moderate temperature and and good soil favour quick growth of plants. Considering the physiography, rainfall, temperature and soil as well as the density of the population it will be clear that this land use system is specially restricted within hill slopes below 1000 metre altitude. Even today in the remote hills of North Eastern India there is no better alternative land use system to swidden cultivation.

The chief characteristics of swidden cultivation as practised by the Wancho are the following:

1. Rotation of fields
2. Use of fire for clearing the land
3. Keeping the land fallow for a number of years for regeneration of forest.
4. Use of human labour as chief input
5. Non-employment of draught animals

6. Use of very crude and simple instruments such as dibbling stick, scrapper etc.
7. Hunting and food gathering are important subsidiary occupations of the swiddeners.

During the winter months (December to February) the trees of the selected forest sites are cut down and are left there to be dried. Occasionally, a few large trees may be left intact, but usually the branches are lopped off and large pieces are removed from the site for fuel. The slash is allowed to dry during the rainless winter months and then burnt during March and April. Dry leaves and small twigs are burnt *in situ* whereas large logs are piled and fired two or three times to ensure complete burning. After one or two showers in April and May weeding is done and then mixed crops are sown by dibbling in the steep slopes with hardly any other preparation of fields. The size of a *Jhum* plot varies between 1.5 to 2.5 hectares for an average family of two adults and three or four children. Several types of crops are grown including maize (corn) and millets. Pulses, beans, mustard, yams, sweat potatoes, chillies, ginger, turmeric and many kinds of vegetables are also raised on the same plot.

All families in the village have their land within a *Jhum* circle where they cultivate their individual plots. In addition, a particular plot of land is cleared by the people of the village and is cultivated on a co-operative basis. The produce of that particular plot of land goes to the chief's house.

Though the Wancho people do not have any measurement of their land, they demarcate their plots by placing some stones in between two plots. They also plant an onion like plant, locally called *Pupa-chinglung* under the stones. The plant produces only one root every year. This plant stands as the last witness in between the plots of land and nobody dare uproot this plant.

Selection of the *Jhum* plots and rituals attached to it

The Wancho people select the *Jhum* field for a particular year in a customary fashion finding out a good omen. They break an egg on their left hand while sitting on a particular plot of land. The position of the broken shells of the egg indicates whether that selection is good or bad. If the position of shells signifies good omen, that plot of land is selected for cultivation. After selection of the plot they perform some rituals before clearing the jungle. The Wancho people locally called it – *Haram Puja*. For this *puja* (worship) they go to their own plot with some poultry droppings. This dropping is mixed with the soil taken from the field and boiled in a bamboo tube. The boiled mixture of soil and poultry excreta is then scattered on the field. It is believed that this ritual helps in warding off insects from the field which would otherwise have destroyed the paddy crop.

The swidden cultivators face many problems. They put in more labour compared to the wet-rice cultivators. The main problem of swidden cultivation is that of clearing the jungle. Till today, the shifting cultivators clear their *Jhum* field in a traditional manner. In the hilly areas they first cut down the jungle and leave it to dry for a month or two. But different parts of the jungle do not dry up at the same time; the jungles which are exposed to the sunlight (Wancho people locally called it *Haham*) dry sooner than the jungles which lie on the reverse side of the hill (locally called *Hadab*). The cultivators find it difficult to burn the jungle evenly for this reason. Sometimes untimely rain destroys a good harvest.

The undulating character of land also poses problem, as seeds can not be scattered uniformly. The farmers cannot maintain the uniformity in the process of sowing the seeds and sometimes they put seeds repeatedly at the same place. As a result some places remain without any seed while at others there may be surplus of seeds.

Land Use and Ownership Pattern

The *Jhum* Land Regulation Act of 1947-1948 gives the tribal population absolute rights over *Jhum* land. The *Jhum* land includes "all lands which any member or members of a village or community have a customary right to cultivate by means of shifting cultivation or to utilise by clearing jungles or grazing livestocks provided that such a village or community is in permanent location". Three types of land ownership are found:

1. Land owned by the village/clan
2. Land owned by the chief
3. Land owned by the individual.

Each village owns the lands surrounding it which its ancestors had originally cleared, or purchased, or inherited. Usually, the land belongs to the clan inhabiting the village rather than to a particular household, for immovable property is not immediately divided even on the death of the common ancestor. However, a family maintains a loose control over that patch of land which it first clears for *Jhum* and reserves claim to revert to its cultivation in the next *Jhum* cycle. Since a man comes back to a particular plot after a gap of 10 years or so he owns at least 10 plots to cultivate by rotation. Persons of an alien clan moving into the village take prior permission of the owner to build a new house and to cultivate at a new site. The individual has a right of use only and is not absolute owner of the plot. The unclaimed forest is the joint property of the clan and an individual may extend his agricultural field by clearing in patches without payment to anybody. However, each family has its own bamboo groves by the side of one's dwelling which are privately owned and kept for making new granaries or field huts when required.

The Wancho recognise four types of land viz. village land, agricultural land, jungle land, and reserved forest land. The village land locally called *hamting* is meant for putting up houses and for making kitchen gardens. Sometimes fruit bearing trees are also grown there. Agricultural land is called *Jang* and is used for growing paddy, millet, maize and other crops. In the Jungle land called *Jang* house building materials like bamboo and palm leaf trees are grown. The reserve forest land is known as *nokling*. Generally, the village land and the agricultural land are used by them.

All Wancho villages have well demarcated boundaries. All lands within the boundary belong to the village community as a whole. Within this overall ownership individual holdings are also there. These may relate to both village land and the cultivable land. Sometimes individual holdings may also be found in the jungle land.

The chief of the village is not the owner of the land although he has the final right of disposal which he does in the interests of the community. The individual holding can be transferred, alienated, sold or mortgaged or given as a gift or leased by the owner only to a person belonging to the same village. No land can be transferred to any outsider or even to a Wancho not belonging to the village. If any land is required to be transferred to person other than members of the village, such a decision can be taken by the community as a whole and not by any individual whatever may be his social position.

Each village has several plots of *Jhum* land which are cultivated in turns. The *Jhum* cycle is around 9 to 10 years depending upon the number of fields. Each field is cultivated for two successive seasons. In the first season, millet is grown and in the second paddy. Individual plots are given to each household in each *Jhum* field. The chief's plot is usually the biggest and the best. Those who do not have plots of land in the *Jhum* field, cultivate on lease basis.

For clearing the chief's field (*Haram*), sowing, harvesting and in other activities at least one member of each family is required to join. For sowing of seeds girls belonging to the Wangsa group also join the girls of the Wangham (royal) group. They jointly go for burning the rubbish. During all these operations the participants are served with rice beer at the *haram* by the women of the royal group.

The arduous tasks of cutting and burning the swidden are undertaken by men while clearing and preparing of the field are primarily the task of women. Each agricultural operation is preceded or followed by some rituals. The millet being the most important crop has a large number of rituals attached to it. Seeds of millet and paddy are sown broadcast while for the other crops seeds are put in holes made with the digging sticks. Sowing is done by experts called *haipa.* It is always done by men; women are excluded from this operation. In the newly prepared fields millets, arum, pulses, chillies, ginger etc. are cultivated and in the previous year's fields *ahu* paddy and other crops are grown. Arum tuber planting by making holes with the digging sticks is called *toa kaili.* It is planted with millet in the same field. Seeds of pulses are also planted like arum. Sesame seeds are sown along with millets in the new fields.

Jhum Cycle

Every village has got 9 to 10 *Jhum* fields and the cycle varies according to the number of fields. After being cultivated for two seasons the land is left fallow so that it may recuperate its fertility. The new *Jhum* field is selected after a divination ceremony. A ritual specialist called *Ngopa* consults the omen by putting a piece of bamboo of particular variety into the fire. This bamboo piece is taken out later and studied with great care. Sometimes another expert *Aupa* reads the omen on an egg. Each field in the *Jhum* cycle has a specific name which is drawn from the nature of the soil or its location. The names of the *Jhum* fields of Pongchaw village are given below together with their possible meaning; it may be noted that with the increasing use of land, the quality of its soil and the quantity of harvest is affected. The same patch of land is described differently at different stages of *Jhum* cycle.

Kham mon: It is a distorted form of the word *Kho-Huan,* which means falling of hair. This name is given to the field which has rich harvest, there is so much to carry on head that the hair begin falling. *Kho-Huan* is thus a metaphoric description of the field: the field which causes baldness.

Chui nam: The field with poor soil and resultant poor harvest is given this name. Those who cultivate such a field are often short of food and have to depend on a kind of wild vegetable called *Chuinam.* So the name *Chuinam* is given to the field.

Loak Kho: Means pushing down of a elephant (*Loak*-elephant, *Kho*-to push down). It is said that once an elephant entered the field and as one side of the land was high and steep it could not get out. The people tried to push the elephant down into the deep gorge but could not. So the land with steep slope bears this designation.

Ju-sap: Land highly infested by rats which damage the crop. The actual name is *Ju Sap* which means "eaten by rats".

Gung Hung: Distorted form of *Nung Hung* which means empty basket. *Nung* or *No* means basket and *Hung* means empty. That means the harvest is so poor that the people sometimes return with empty baskets.

Abaw: High land where previously birds used to chirp loudly. The twittering and chirping of birds is called *abaw.*

Gumba: *Gumba* means no food to eat. The land is not fertile and so harvest is poor. People do not get sufficient crop. So they think their one year's labour is wasted.

The *Jhum* cycle of Pongchaw village as recorded in 1959 is given below:

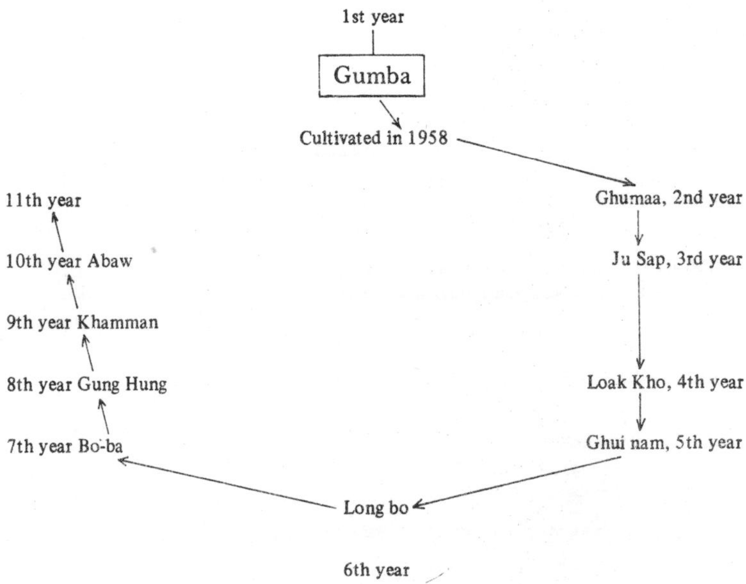

The Agricultural Calendar

The Wancho remain busy in their agricultural work for almost the whole year except for two months, May and June. During these two months they generally undertake other pursuits like selling their surplus grains or arts and crafts in the plains. Alternatively, they do daily wage labour wherever available. Their annual routine of agricultural activities and the main crops they grow are given below in Table 1 and 2.

The Wancho do not use any insecticides or pesticides since crop disease and pests are very rare. The main reason of this is burning of the *Jhum* fields before sowing. However, once in a while the plants are attacked by pests; in such a case the Wancho collect them in bamboo tubes and burn them.

Wet rice cultivation is not popular among the Wancho as suitable land and assured irrigation facilities are not available. People in many villages, however, know techniques of wet rice cultivation. In some villages the people are reluctant to take to it for the river banks are supposed to be haunted by evil spirit called *kashi-jogan* (a female mendicant from Kashi). At the places believed to be haunted, people make offerings to the spirit and refrain from drinking water at that spot.

Table 1. Calendar of Agricultural Activities

Months	*Major Activities*
January	Preparation of field and sowing of millet and maize seeds. Planting of arum and tapioca.
February	Preparation of field for ahu-paddy. Sewing of millet and maize seeds and planting arum and tapioca continue.
March	Sowing of ahu-paddy seeds stars. Planting of tapioca continue.
April	Sowing of ahu-paddy seeds continue.
May	No agricultural activity for men. Women take up weeding of paddy and millet.
June	Same as in May.
July	Harvesting of millet, maize and arum starts.
August	Harvesting work continues.
September	Harvesting of paddy and tapioca starts.
October	Harvesting of paddy and tapioca continues. Preparation of field for millet, arum tapioca and maize starts.
November	Harvesting of tapioca continues.
December	Preparation of field for paddy starts.

Table 2. Cropwise Agricultural Operations

Name of Crops	*Preparation of field*	*Seed Sowing*	*Harvesting*
1. Paddy	December to February.	March to April	September to October.
2. Millet	October to mid January	Mid January to mid February.	Middle of July to end of August.
3. Arum	– do –	– do –	– do –
4. Tapioca	– do –	February and March.	September to November.
5. Maize (Corn)	– do –	Mid January to mid February.	July/August

View of a "Jhum" field – Wancho area.

Clearing the jungle for "Jhum" cultivation.

Courtesy : Directorate of Information
and Public Relations,
Arunachal Pradesh.

View of "Jhum" field.

Wancho men working in the "Jhum" field.

In most villages, the grain is pulled out of the plants by hand. In some villages the ears of the paddy are cut with a small knife or *dao*. Nowadays sickles are also being used in some villages. Threshing is not required if the grain is pulled out by hand. In other cases threshing is done by trampling on the plants near the farm house on a piece of ground cleared for the purpose. It is done by men only. After threshing the grains are brought home in conical bamboo baskets and stored in the granaries. Some of the grains are preserved for next year's sowing. Seeds are rarely imported from outside. To save the seeds from insects they are thoroughly dried in the sun before preservation. Seeds are preserved in old bamboo tubes or in earthen pots.

People's Perception and Attitude Towards Swiddening

Although swiddening practices have attracted the attention of social scientists in the areas it occurs, we do not get any idea of the people's perception of swiddening practices and the extent of their attachment to it. An attempt has been made in the following pages through holistic intensive field study to find out people's reactions to the entire process as such. The exercise covered the swiddeners themselves, the village leaders, the *Anchal Samiti* members from the area and some of the Development Officers working among the people in the five villages selected for the study.

The five villages were all within the same ecological area characterised by swidden cultivation as the predominant mode of livelihood. The villages were chosen purposively to examine existing variations in swidden practices and also to study those sections of the population who have changed over to settled wet rice cultivation. In three villages namely, Pongchow, Mintong and Niausa people were wholly devoted to swidden cultivation, while in Zedua and Rusa some families have gone over to settled cultivation.

The holistic study was intended to find out the population and its resource base, comparative productivity of various kinds of land use, the extent of subsistence and cash crop farming and other means of livelihood, household resource management and the quality of life of the swidden cultivation in the villages. Since no efforts have been made by the Government to settle the Wancho in permanent cultivation, such a programme has been studied in respect of another tribe, the Digaru-Mishmi in the neighbouring district of Lohit. In the Wancho area, the Forest Department is carrying out some programmes for the control of swidden cultivation. Details of the programme and its impact on the tribals will be discussed in another section.

In this section, we seek to explore the perceptions of swidden cultivators regarding their commitment to swiddening practices, shifting of household, the fallow interval, the evils of swidden cultivation, the main problems connected with it, their priorities for attaining a better quality of life and whether swidden cultivation should be allowed to continue. They were also urged to give suggestions for improving the swiddening system.

Some of these questions were posed before the village leaders and the members of *Anchal Samitis.* Their reactions are extremely important as they are the opinion leaders and decision makers in regard to all activity in their areas. Almost all of them are also swiddeners but they are more exposed to the development ideas and are keen to work for the betterment of the lot of the people. A schedule was also administered to the Development Officers who were working in the area for quite some time. They are expected to be well conversant with the local physiography, resources and the problems of development. Their reactions to some of the questions posed to them are, therefore, extremely important.

Since swiddening is the main concern of this study, it is useful to have an idea about the differential perception of its evils among the ordinary swiddeners, village leaders, *Anchal Samiti* members and the development officers.

The percentages of their responses are given in Table 3.

It is seen that the responses in the category "those who agree that swiddening is bad for environment" goes on increasing as we proceed from the swiddeners to the Development Officers. It is significant that very few of the actual swiddeners have the realisation that it is bad for the environment. Even these admitted of the adverse effect only when they were further probed. The increment in this category from the swiddeners to the village leaders is not very large. It is thus clear that the village leaders who take all important

Table 3. Differential Perception of the Evils of Swiddening

Statements	*Agree*				*Disagree*				*Do not know*			
	SW	*VL*	*ASM*	*DO*	*DW*	*VL*	*ASM*	*DO*	*SW*	*VL*	*ASM*	*DO*
Bad for environment.	10	25	60	61	67	71	40	8	13	4	x	31
Causes soil erosion	20.5	96	80	69	13.5	0	20	x	66	4	x	31
Gives lower yield than permanent cultivation	61	68	100	69	5	4	x	x	34	28	x	31

SW – Swiddeners; ASM – Anchal Samiti Members;
VL – Village Leaders; DO – Development Officers.

decisions regarding cultivation and other matters have a poor realisation that swiddening is bad for the environment. At the level of the *Anchal Samiti* members this realisation is very much more since they are more educated and also more exposed to outside influences than the village leaders. Even in this category there is a substantial percentage of people who disagree with this proposition. The response in the Development Officer's category is rather surprising. Some of the officers refrained from commenting on the adverse effects of swiddening by answering "do not know". It is hard to believe that they were ignorant. Perhaps they did not want to comment or publicly express a view favouring swiddening.

One of the evils of swiddening is that it causes soil erosion. However, the large mass of swiddeners does not agree with this view as a matter of fact, two thirds of the swiddeners do not know whether this is so. Among the village leaders, however, the realisation of the adverse consequence of swiddening is almost complete. Only 4 per cent do not know whether this is so. It seems that they are convinced about this aspect but they are not able to do anything about it on account of the lack of a suitable alternative. The percentage among *Anchal Samiti* members is surprisingly less in this category than those of the village leaders. It is also intriguing that the percentage is even less among the Development Officers. Nearly one third among them are non-committal since they do not know whether swiddening causes soil erosion. This response like the earlier one, reveals their unwillingness to come out openly in favour of or against swiddening.

The responses regarding the third aspect of the question that the yield in swiddening is much lower than in permanent cultivation, are very clear. All categories of respondents have a clear realisation of this fact. The percentage among swiddeners and village leaders is nearly the same. Among the *Anchal Samiti* members this knowledges is all pervading. Among the Development Officers the response is the same as in the earlier queries, since almost one third of them said that they do not know whether the yield is lower than in permanent cultivation. This betrays either their gross ignorance or inability to speak the truth.

The Swiddeners

Majority of the respondents are of higher age group. The following table shows the age distribution of the respondents:

Table 4. Age Distribution of Swiddeners

Age Interval	*Frequency*
15 – 20	7
21 – 30	40
31 – 40	41
41 – 50	34
51 above	34
Total	156

Ever since this area came under the purview of administration, efforts have been made to spread education among people in this area. The Wancho have no liking for education. They do not have sufficient motivation for it. Government has been trying to establish many educational institutions even in the remote places which are difficult to reach. The literacy rate is very low among the people. The following table shows the education of the respondents:

Table 5. Break up of Swiddeners According to Educational Levels.

Standard of Education	*Frequency*
None	140
Primary	15
Secondary	1
Total	156

From the above table it is clear that out of 156 respondents only one respondent had education up to the secondary level. 15 respondents have education up to primary level. 140 respondents have got no education.

Swidden cultivation is the only method of agriculture of the Wancho people. They are practising it ever since they settled in this region. Agriculture is the primary and main occupation of the Wancho. They have their own land for cultivation in each *Jhum* cycle. There are only a few cases where people took land from others on lease. Among the respondents 146 had their own land, while only 10 had taken land on lease.

Generally the Wancho do not have a standard measure of land and do not know how much land each family cultivates every year. But it is observed that they cultivate approximately 2 to 8 acres of land. The size of the plot differs from family to family. A large family generally cultivates a larger field. The following table shows the land under cultivation (in acres).

Table 6. Distribution of Swiddeners by Landholding

Land (in acres)	*Frequency*
0 – 1	0
2 – 4	24
5 – 8	62
9 above	70
Total	156

1 acre = 0.40,468 hectares; 1 hectare = 2.47,106 acres

As the table shows, the majority of respondents cultivates more than nine acres of land. 62 families cultivate 5 to 8 acres, and only 24 families cultivate 2 to 4 acres of land.

For the whole year the Wancho keep busy in various agricultural operations. In addition to their agricultural work the male members of the family sometimes go for casual labour. Out of 156 total respondents 19 worked as casual labour. They are employed either by the Central Public Works Development or in the Forest Department.

The annual income of the Wancho people is very low. Nearly 75 per cent of the total population of the five villages is below the poverty line. They have to depend upon what they get out of their agricultural produce. But their existing agricultural system cannot provide them for their basic needs. In times of scarcity they depend only upon arum and tapioca.

101 of the respondents have an income above Rs.500/- (income including agriculture and labour). 46 families have an income within the range of Rs.401-500 and only 9 families are in the income bracket of Rs.301-400.

Swidden cultivators shift their plots every year. After one year of cultivation the fertility of the land is exhausted. So they shift to another plot the following year. Generally the people leave a plot fallow for a period of about 8 to 10 years. But sometimes due to the scarcity of land people return to a plot even before a lapse of 8 years.

It was found that the fallow interval of the bulk of respondents (95) is 10-12 years. 49 respondents out of 156 left their land fallow for a period of 7 to 9 years and only 12 respondents leave the land fallow for 4 to 6 years.

In some places close to the plains of Assam, people enthusiastically go in for wet-rice cultivation. But in the places of high altitude with steep hills and uneven land the practice of wet-rice cultivation is impossible. There are very few plots of cultivable plain land with available water supply in the Wancho area for people to switch over to wet-rice cultivation.

In our sample there are only 27 respondents who practise wet-rice cultivation. These are particularly from Rusa and Zedua village, where they have got some plain land close to the plains border of Assam and in the river bed of Tissing river respectively.

For the agricultural development of the Wancho people Government provides some facilities in terms of subsidies. Paddy seeds, potato, chemical fertiliser, tools etc. are provided by the government. These inputs have yielded richer harvest, and a better income.

The Wancho cultivate other crops besides paddy. The main crops are paddy, millet, maize, arum, tapioca, local oat, maskalai etc. The following table gives a picture of their important crops.

Table 7. Important Crops Raised by Swiddeners

Crops order	*Paddy*	*Millet*	*Maize*	*Arum & Topioca*	*Local Oat, Chilli, Ginger, Maskalai*
1	156	x	x	x	x
2	x	151	3	2	x
3	x	5	91	27	33
4	x	x	62	127	123

It is clear from the above that all the respondents give importance to paddy growing. But the production of paddy in this area is not adequate and people have to depend upon other crops like tapioca, arum, millet, etc. Millet and tapioca are also used for making beer.

As already stated, swidden cultivation is the traditional method of cultivation of the Wancho and they are continuing it from the time of their forefathers. There was no other means of their livelihood except swidden cultivation. Generally, the children of swiddeners begin to help in farming around the age of 10.

It is interesting to note that most of the respondents were quite unaware of any damages caused by swidden cultivation. Year after year, the swidden cultivators make use of forest resources by felling trees and burning them, in order to make the soil suitable for cultivation. But they do not perceive this as destruction of forests. In the absence of any other viable alternative in their ecological setting, they regard swiddening as the appropriate mode of production of food.

We also asked the respondents about the problems connected with swidden cultivation. The main problem in swiddening experienced by the swiddeners relates to the clearing of the jungle. There are also some other problems like sowing seeds evenly, problem of harvesting etc. In the hills people first cut down the vegetation and they leave it to dry for a month or two. When the felled plants dry up they set fire. But the problem is that all the trees do not dry equally, and at the same time.

Moreover, the undulating land makes difficult even and uniform scattering of seeds. The farmers cannot maintain the uniformity in the process of sowing the seeds and sometimes they throw seeds repeatedly at the same place instead of throwing them equally all around.

Swiddeners' opinion regarding resettlement and *in-situ* development were enquired into. All but 6 respondents were found to be averse to any kind of resettlement. Old people do not like to go outside in search of other occupations. It may be due to their natural attachment with their own land. Illiterate tribals cannot think of development of the village residing in the remote areas far removed from advanced society. But the younger generation which is in close touch with developed populations is not averse to sugestions for resettlement.

Village Leaders

Thirty-two village leaders from the five villages under study were interviewed with the help of a schedule. 15 out of 32 village leaders were in the age group of 31-40. Five of them belonged to the 21-30 age-group and nine to the 41-50 age group. Thus, the bulk of the village leaders came from the mature and middle age group. However, only 8 of them had some education, 4 of them were educated up to the primary level and 4 up to the secondary level. Almost all of them were educated in their own village and all the village leaders belonged to the villages of their birth. All of them were also land owners and did not hoid any land on lease from anyone else. However, some of them occasionally supplemented their income through working as daily labourers in road maintenance work or in different kinds of activities organised by the Forest Department.

Twenty out of the 32 village leaders owned between 1 to 10 acres of land and 11 owned between 11 to 20 acres. Only one person had about 50 acres. Four of these leaders had an annual income of less then Rs.500/-. The rest (28) had an income above Rs.500/-. The actual area under cultivation of 28 village leaders was in the "holding" group of 1 to 5 acres. Only 4 cultivated holdings over 6 acres. The fallow interval in case of 21 was 10-12 years and for the rest was 7-9 years. In two villages, some of the leaders had some land under permanent cultivation. There were 8 such leaders out of whom 7 cultivated between 1 to 5 acres and only 1 held between 6 to 10 acres. Modernization of agriculture was only possible in case of permanent cultivation. Out of 8 village leaders who were engaged in wet-rice cultivation only 2 used power-tiller for some time. One of the power-tillers had broken down in a field close to the river-bed in village Zedua. However, the Agriculture Department had provided some facilities to 15 out of 32 village leaders. All the 15 received paddy seeds, 12 received potato seeds, 8 received chemical fertilizers, and 4 were given simple agricultural tools.

Only 6 of the village leaders had been able to increase their yield and thereby, their income on account of the use of new techniques and other inputs in agriculture. The increased yield was due to the use of improved seeds and power-tillers. Only one leader attributed it to better technical knowledge. Another person believed that it was due to the use of chemical fertilizer.

As in the case of the responses of swiddeners, paddy continued to be the most important crop followed by millet, maize, arum and tapioca. Table 8 gives an idea of crops in order of importance.

All the village leaders were engaged in swiddening. 22 of the village leaders had begun helping their parents in this work between the age of 11 to 15. Ten others had joined this work at an even more tender age. These people have not changed their place of residence even though they continually shift their plots for cropping every year. There are only 4 leaders who had moved their residence once.

Three of them moved on account of lack of accommodation in the old house, and another had to move because his previous house caught fire and was gutted.

Most of them do not remember when they got some government aid for their agricultural pursuits. Of the 15 who had received the government aid, 7 could not record the year, 8 of them were able to do so as given in Table 9.

Table 8. Crops in Order of Importance

Crops	*Order*			
	1	*2*	*3*	*4*
Paddy	32	–	–	–
Millet		29	3	–
Maize		3	27	2
Arum Tapioca Chilly Ginger			2	30 –

Table 9. Year when Government Aid Received.

Year	*No. of people who received aid*
1965	2
1970	3
1977	2
1978	1
Do not remember	7
Not received	17
Total	32

The village leaders are all agreed that in swiddening the biggest problem is the clearance of forest. Some of them are also aware of the problems of sowing seeds evenly. They also experience difficulty in putting fertilizers.

In spite of the difficulties in swidden cultivation, only 3 of the village leaders were in favour of joining a resettlement colony for taking up permanent cultivation. The overwhelming majority wanted something to be done for development in the places where they lived.

The village leaders were asked to indicate their preference for a number of items considered necessary for the development. The following table lists these preferences:

Table 10. Preference of Items for Development

	1	*2*	*3*	*4*	*5*	*6*
Better yield	1	4	4	15	8	x
Health & Medical facilities	x	5	13	6	7	1
School	16	4	6	3	3	x
More food	3	4	3	4	8	10
More mechanised farming methods	12	13	3	3	x	2
Better housing	x	2	3	1	6	20

It is significant to note that the school has been given first preference by as many as 16 or 50 per cent of the village leaders. Improved farming methods has been preferred by 12 village leaders. In the second preference, improved farming has the largest number of respondents. Better health and better housing appear to be least important considerations. Better yield and more food are also regarded as insignificant.

29 respondents wanted swidden cultivation to continue. When asked about the reasons, 14 of them said that this is because no plain land was available for wet-rice cultivation. Six of them believed that there was no alternative to swiddening; three of them wanted to stick to it since it was a part of their cultural tradition; four of them opted for it because of their emotional attachment to the way of life revolving around swidden cultivation.

The village leaders were asked to give suggestions for the improvement of the swiddening system. Their suggestions are noted below together with the number of respondents opting for each.

Table 11. Suggestions for Improvement of Swiddening

1. Better farming method	20
2. Technical knowledge	3
3. Supply of H.V.V. seeds	4
4. Chemical fertilizer	6
5. Supply of machine tools	5
6. Do not know	4

It is thus clear that most of the village leaders are in favour of better farming methods in swiddening. They are all keen that the best advantage should be taken of the harsh environment from which there is no escape.

Anchal Samiti Members

Anchal Samitis have been constituted in Arunachal Pradesh to involve the local people in the task of development. They are elective bodies comprising representatives from a group of villagers. They are charged with the all round development of villages by providing for education, communication, agriculture and medical facilities. Ten *Anchal Samiti* members from the areas covered by the study villages were interviewed with the help of a schedule to know their attitudes towards swiddening. These are the elite in Wancho society. Their views prevail in all matters related to the administration and development, since they are the elected representatives of the people.

8 of the 10 persons interviewed were members and 2 were Vice Presidents of the *Anchal Samitis;* 6 of them were in the age group of 31 to 40 and 3 were past 40. Only one of them was below 30. Thus the *Anchal Samiti* members interviewed were all comparatively young. However, 6 of them were completely illiterate and 4 had attended school up to the primary level. Six of them were involved with the swiddeners for more than 25 years, and 2 of them were involved with them for about 20 years. Thus nearly all of them had long experience of living with the swiddeners and being acquainted with their attitudes and problems.

An attempt was made to see their perception of the views of the swiddeners on those same statements. The responses given in the following table indicate that they have imputed their own views on the swiddeners. While the bulk of the swiddeners are unaware of the damages of swidden, the *Anchal Samiti* members acknowledge that such practice leads to soil erosion. Some of them realize that the yields are lower than in permanent cultivation but others do not know anything about it since they have no experience of permanent cultivation.

Table 12. *Anchal Samiti* Member's Perception of Swiddeners View on Evils of Soil Erosion.

	Yes	*No*	*Do not know*
1. Swidden cultivation causes soil erosion.	9	x	1
2. Swidden cultivation gives lower yield than permanent cultivation.	5	x	5

The Samiti members were asked about the alternative occupation the swiddeners would like to be provided with. In this they have reflected their own preferences. All of them have given business as a first preference and 9 out of 10 have given preference for white collar jobs. This reflects the preference of the educated young men all over Arunachal Pradesh.

They were also asked whether they would like their children to continue as swiddeners. 60 per cent of these replied in the negative. Asked about the reasons for this response, they supplied the following:

Table 13. Reasons for Not Continuing as Swiddeners

1. Once their children go for other job they will not like to do farming.	1
2. It is troublesome	3
3. To educate them	2
4. Population pressure in land stimulated the villagers to adopt some other means of livelihood.	1

The four respondents who wanted their children to continue swidden argued that more manpower is needed, and if the children were to drift, their agriculture would suffer.

It is seen that 3 of them want to change over since swiddening is troublesome. The pressure of population on land is increasing and at least one of the members feels the need to adopt some other means for livelihood. Two of them want their children to be educated and thus do not want to socialize them in swidden culture.

The members feel that the swiddeners prefer *in-situ* development to resettlement. The main problems of resettlement as viewed by the members in order of their importance are listed below.

Table 14. Problems Perceived in Resettlement

1. Problem of shifting with hearth and home	10
2. Lack of fertile land	6
3. Natural attachment to their own land	9
4. Superstitious beliefs	1

All the members feel that the main problem is to convince people to shift their homes as they are deeply attached to their own land. Added to this is the non-availability of level land for wet-rice cultivation. The leaders did not feel that superstitious beliefs are a hurdle to resettlement programmes.

The respondents were asked to highlight the main problems of *in-situ* development. Their responses are given in the following table:

Table 15. Problems of *In-Situ* Development

1. Problem of communication	10
2. Mass media	1
3. Illiteracy	9
4. Ecological peculiarities	1
5. Customary laws	2

The main problem in *in-situ* development is that of communication, since the villages are located in relatively inaccessible hill slopes or hill tops. Illiteracy among the swiddeners is a handicap; lack of education makes them stick to old tradition. However, only two of the respondents felt that customary laws prevent *in-situ* development.

The *Samiti* members were asked to rank 6 items in order of their importance in the context of development. Their responses are given below:

Table 16. Ranking of Development Items

Rank / *Items*	*1*	*2*	*3*	*4*	*5*	*6*
Better yield	1	2	x	5	2	x
Health & Medical facilities	x	x	6	3	1	x
School	6	1	3	x	x	x
More food	x	x	x	1	4	5
More mechanised farming methods	3	6	1	x	x	x
Better housing	x	1	x	1	3	5
Total	10	10	10	10	10	10

It may be noted that school has been given top priority by the bulk of the members. Next to it is improved farming technology. Better yield is the fourth preference, while health and medical facilities are given the third preference. Availability of more food has been relegated to the fifth and sixth preference along with better housing. It is thus clear that the people are not very much concerned about food and housing. The first priority given to the school is indicative of their desire for a better quality of life which can only be possible with education.

In order to know their attitude to diversification of crops the *Samiti* members were asked to name the crops other then paddy which they grow in the *Jhum* fields. They were also asked to mention, which of the crops they wanted besides paddy. To this question almost all listed millet, tapioca, arum, and maize.

Development Officers

In Wancho area, as also in other areas, a number of State Government Officers are engaged in various kinds of developmental activities. Their task is to implement government policies and programmes with the co-operation of the local people. Being stationed in that area they are generally conversant with the problems of the people; and they are also familiar with people's attitude towards various developmental activities. In view of their experience and interest in the area an attempt was made to assess their views with the help of a schedule. These officers are at various levels such as Extra Assistant Commissioner (EAC), Block Development Officer (BDO), Circle Officers, Agricultural Officers and Village Level Workers (VLW). A total of 13 such officers were interviewed. 10 of them were in the age group of 20 to 35, only 3 were above 35. All of them were educated, 8 up to the secondary level and 5 were holders of university degrees. 8 of them had been involved with the swidden cultivators for 1 to 10 years and 5 of them had been working for a longer time in that area. The higher officers like EAC, BDO, and Circle Officer were concerned with the all-round development of the village including administrative, judicial and other activities. The Agriculture Officer and the VLW were engaged in providing agricultural inputs and looking after agricultural extension work.

The development officers were asked about the views of swiddeners regarding some of the detrimental effects of the practice of swidden cultivation. Their reactions are given below:

Table 17. Development Officers' Perception of Swiddeners' View on Evils of Swiddening

	Yes	*No*	*Do not know*
1. Swidden cultivation causes soil erosion.	13	x	x
2. Swidden cultivation gives lower yield than permanent cultivation.	10	x	3

They were also asked about the preference of the swiddeners for alternative occupations. Their perception of swiddeners' preferences is tabulated below:

Table 18. Development Officers' Perception of Swiddeners' Preference for Alternative Occupations.

	Order of Preference			
Alternatives	*1*	*2*	*3*	*4*
Business	9	4	–	–
White Collar Job	4	9	–	–
Casual Labour	–	–	13	–

It is clear that the first preference is for business followed by white collar job. Casual labour appears to be the last recourse.

The development officers think that the bulk of the swiddeners would like to continue with their traditional economy. The main reason for this is the topography of the land they occupy and also their being very conservative. Those of them that would like to change to settled cultivation would do so to get an increased yield and thereby improve their standard of living. They are also fed up with swiddening because it is very troublesome.

The development officers feel that *in-situ* development is largely desired by swidden cultivators. The reasons for this are listed in the following table:

Table 19. Reasons for Preference for *In-Situ* Development

	1	*2*	*3*	*4*
Natural attachment to his own village	5	x	5	3
Superstitious beliefs	x	9	2	2
Problem of shifting with hearth and home	x	4	2	7
Lack of available fertile land	8	x	4	1

It is seen that the most important reasons for not opting for resettlement are natural attachment to the village and also lack of available fertile land. Superstitious beliefs do not really produce a hurdle in resettlement as they have been relegated to the second order in importance.

The problems of *in-situ* development were also enquired from the development officers. Their responses are given in the table below:

Table 20. Problems of *In-Situ* Development

	Preferences		
	1	*2*	*3*
1. Problem of communication	13	x	x
2. Insufficient education	x	7	x
3. Problem of mass media	x	x	5
4. Rigidity of the social norms	x	x	2
5. Illiteracy of the general masses	x	1	4
6. Lack of awareness of the villagers	x	5	2

It is obvious that to the development officers the problem of communication is the most important. All inputs, supplies and services have to be reached the inaccessible villages, some of which may be small in size. Education is the next most important problem together with their lack of awareness of their environment.

The development officers were asked about their perception of the swiddeners' views about improving their life styles. Their reactions are given in the following table:

Table 21. Development Officer's Perceptions of Swiddeners' Views on their Life Style

	1	*2*	*3*	*4*	*5*	*6*
Better yield	3	4	2	3	x	1
Health & Medical facilities	x	x	5	2	2	4
Education	1	4	3	2	3	x
More food	8	x	1	3	1	x
More mechanised farming methods	1	5	2	2	2	1
Better housing	x	x	x	1	5	7

It is clear that their perception is different from that of *Anchal Samiti* members. The bulk of them view more food and better yields as the most important items for achieving a better standard of living. In the second preference importance has been given to more advanced farming methods, better yield and education.

The change in responses may be due to the fact that 6 out of the 13 respondents are directly engaged in agricultural development.

It is seen by the development officers also that the swiddeners want to grow some other crops besides paddy. These crops are millet, arum and tapioca.

The officers revealed that they do not receive any suggestions from the swiddeners for improving their own programmes. Nine of them did not receive any suggestion whatever. The five who received suggestions said that these were related to better farming, supply of seeds, and tools for agriculture free of cost.

Swidden Control Programme

Swiddening is a way of life with the tribal people in most parts of Arunachal Pradesh. The pattern of cultivation in this area is governed not only by the physiography and soil fertility but also by the whole social, historical, and environmental setting of the people. Their effort is to get the maximum return possible from the harsh ecology in which they have been placed by nature. This old age practice is in harmony with nature. But the growing pressure of the population and the reduction in the fallow interval has forced the people to think about other alternatives. Since people are attached to their hearth and home and to the village they would not like to go far away in search of plain land which is suitable for wet-rice cultivation. We have, therefore, to think in terms of *in-situ* development rather than that of resettlement. As a part solution to the problem, the Indian Council of Agricultural Research Station at Shillong has suggested partial terracing with horticulture and forestry development on the upper slope. It is desirable to keep cereal cultivation to a maximum and encourage horticulture and other perennial crops. These would cause less damage to the environment. The local economy may be developed by intensively growing horticulture and plantation crops.

The Forest Department of the Arunachal Pradesh Government has taken up the swidden cultivation control programme under the Central Government scheme "Soil, Water and Tree Preservation in the Himalayas" supplemented by state inputs. The experience gained as a result of various programmes taken up under this scheme indicated that it was necessary to formulate an integrated area development approach which could claim the co-operation of the local people in a much better way. Since Wancho area has been almost wholly devoted to swidden cultivation, it was decided to take up four out of the six projects in the State in this area. The projects are located at Mintong, Bonia, Nissa and Longkhow in the Tirap district. The unit for each project could not be on natural area like a water-shed or a catchment basin. Land had to be obtained for demonstration work. Since land was under the control of village chief the village had to be treated as a development unit.

One of the oldest projects under this scheme starting in 1979-1980 had been taken up in Mintong village. After considerable persuasion the chief of the village agreed to give about 10 sq. km. of fallow area. The rainfall in this village is nearly 2600 mm. per year. As a matter of fact no month passes without any shower. The temperature ranges from 6° Celsius in January to 30° Celsius in July. The area brought under the project varies in elevation from 1000 metres to 1600 metres. The slope varies from 20° to 80°. The area is covered with grass and shurbs and scattered with heavily lopped trees. The *jhum* cycle is of 11 years. Each family takes up cultivation in about 1 to 1½ hectares in 4 to 5 plots. Certain patches containing original forests are located on hill tops. These are covered by the eastern Himalayan sub tropical wet hill forests. Grasses of different varieties are also found. The people grow crops of hill paddy, millet, arum and tapioca. The food that they grow does not suffice for the whole year. Some of the people take up wage labour by working for road maintenance under the Central Public Works Department. April to June is a very critical period because by that time their food resources are generally depleted.

Before the programme was started, a local Committee was constituted with the village chief (the *Gaonbura*) and certain other village leaders as members. The development programmes to be taken up were discussed in the Committee with the hope that this will ensure the co-operation of the villagers. To begin with, a survey was conducted of the land use. Though there are three perennial streams it was seen that there is no suitable level of gentle slope land on the banks of the streams for developing irrigated paddy fields. Out of the total area of 1000 hectares, 300 hectares was expected to be brought under cash crop. The rest of the area was left for fruits and forestry crops.

The main object of the programme was to wean the people from swidden cultivation practices through better crop cultivation which would yield higher income and enable them to sustain a higher standard of living much above the poverty line. Quick growing cash crops like big cardamom, coffee, medicinal plants, and spices were considered well suited for the programme.

Big cardamom was selected for Mintong taking into account the local conditions. It starts fruiting from the third year onward reaching the maximum in the sixth year and continues for about 15 years. The area planted under the big cardamom is to be distributed at the rate of 2 hectares for all the households in the village and each family is expected to get an income of at least Rs.5000 from the sixth year. In selected areas, turmeric will be grown as an inter crop till big cardamom starts yielding and this will further augment their income. The harvesting and marketing of this cash crop will be undertaken by Forest Department in order to ensure a reasonable return to the people.

In order to interest the people in the programme from the beginning an effort was made to provide employment for one adult member in each household throughout the year whenever they were not engaged in swidden operations and were available for work. Labour intensive work like road construction, soil conservation, and afforestation were organised without using mechanical equipment like bulldozers and tractors. On account of such work the annual income of the average household is expected to increase from Rs.1000 to Rs.3000. Efforts were also made to provide for the minimum needs of the people viz. food, fire-wood, housing, education, health, and nutrition.

In Mintong village which is located on hill top, women mainly collect water and fire-wood from the forest area on the banks of Tissa river or one of its tributaries. In order to save them from this drudgery, fuel wood plantations were proposed to be raised in 300 hectares in the upper slopes near their village to provide them with fire-wood from the 6th year onward. In the remaining area of 400 hectares seedlings of fruit trees and useful timber species will also be planted to provide additional food and fuel supply to the people. It was also expected that the forestry plantation raised in the area will provide the necessary shade, thus changing the micro climate of the area. Before the work actually started the villagers posed the problem of communication and insisted that a link road of 1 km. should be made as soon as possible. Along with the road other means of employment like pasture development, afforestation, terracing, prevention of soil erosion, planting of fruits and other useful seedlings were taken up. The terrace method of cultivation along with contour bunding was propagated in the area.

A private person was allowed to open a shop near the village to supply grocery and other articles at a reasonable rate. A government primary school was also started for the children of the village. The "Food-For-Work Programme" was taken up in order to provide adequate quantity of rice. The scheme became popular because through it people were able to get rice at Rs.1.62 paise per kilogram as compared to the market rate of Rs.2/- per kilogram.

In the year 1980-1981, the programmes of the earlier years were continued with higher targets. Small plantations of black pepper, tea and fruit trees like pear *(nashpati)* were raised. A first aid Centre under the supervision of a qualified person was also opened to provide people with essential medicines. However, "Food-For-Work Programme" could not be continued due to difficulty in procurement of rice on account of the "Assam agitation" on the issue of foreign nationals which has gone on for a number of years. During this year construction of three small ponds for collection of rain water and for pisciculture was also taken up. Four persons from the village who were opium addicts were sent to the rehabilitation Centre to wean them away from opium. The local grocery shop was converted into a fair price shop to supply rice, sugar, kerosene and other essential items at controlled rates. In the year 1981-1982 large areas were expected to be planted with big cardamom, forest and fruit crops. Tokopalm was planted in selected localities to provide leaves for thatching and other purposes. Under the guidance of the Fishery Department a pisciculture project was taken up for which there is a ready market at Longding. The Animal Husbandry

Department initiated a piggery development programme. Efforts to bring drinking water through pipes are also being made. Some more persons are expected to be weaned from opium. Local handicrafts like pottery, grass bead garland making is also being encouraged and marketing facilities are being provided for these.

The expenditure made by the Forest Department on various items together with the physical target proposed to be achieved during the year 1979-1980, 1980-1981 and 1981-1982 are detailed below:

Table 22.—Budget for Forest Operations

Year	*Item*	*Physical*	*Target Financial in Rs.*
1	*2*	*3*	*4*
1979-80	Land use survey	1.2 km	800
	Terracing critically eroded agricultural land.	3 ha	2,080
	Pasture development	3 ha	1,488
	Afforestation	25 ha	37,317
	Raising seedlings	10,000	2,000
	Stabilisation of slips	2 ha	3,200
	Bench terracing (higher slopes)	5 ha	10,000
	Building (OB Type)	4	20,000
	Road construction (part)	0.3 km	3,000
	Other items (stationery, stores etc.)		19,182
		Total	99,066
1980-81	Extension work	4 sq km	800
	Land-use survey	3 sq km	400
	Pasture development (maintenance)	3 ha	800
	Afforestation	122 ha	158,681
	Raising seedlings	7,000	1,750
	Bench terracing	7.15 ha	8,864
	Bench terracing (higher slopes)	4.75 ha	9,584
	Water storage pond	3	21,520
	Tea plantation, including terracing	0.3 ha	12,088
	Big cardamom plantation	6.25 ha	18,472
	Black pepper plantation	1.2 ha	3,792
	Nursery for cash crops and other species	1 ha	28,290
	Fruit plants	1,500	2,100
	Avenue plantation	348	1,728
	Road construction	0.9 km	15,472
	Building construction (OB Type)	3	15,000
	Other items (stationery, stores, vehicle maintenance).	..	61,659
		Total	361,000

Contd. . .

Table 22. *(Continued)*

Year	*Item*	*Physical*	*Target Financial in Rs.*
1	*2*	*3*	*4*
1981-82	Extension work	7 km	1,400
	Land use survey and preparation of working plan	6 km	4,200
	Terracing eroded agricultural lands	10 km	15,000
	Afforestation works	50 km	100,000
	Supply seedlings to farmers	20,000	5,000
	Stabilisation of slips	12 ha	19,200
	Contour bunding	18 ha	5,400
	Bench terracing		
	(a) lower slope	12 ha	14,400
	(b) higher slope	10 ha	20,000
	Water storage tank works	5	83,000
	Big cardamom plantation	30 ha	120,000
	Nursery for cash crops and others	..	30,000
	Fruit plants	1,000	3,000
	Road works	1 km	30,000
	Buildings (OB Type)	3	18,000
	Other items (vehicle maintenance, stores, stationery etc.)	..	71,400
		Total	540,000

It is seen that the expenditure made in the three years was to the tune of Rs.99,066, Rs.361,000 and Rs.540,000 respectively. The total impact by development indicators can now be examined. The programme has included setting up of a primary school which has enrolled 38 children. The fair price shop has made essential commodities like rice, salt and sugar available to the people at cheap rates. A health centre with a trained para-medical staff has also been provided. A one kilometre road from the main road to the plantation area has been built. Employment was provided to more than 200 people in both farm and non-farm work. Efforts were made to eradicate opium addiction among some persons. In the "Food-For-Work Programme", rice was supplied to the people. All these items reflect remarkable efforts on the part of the Forest Department to attract the tribals to their main programme of introducing horticulture and perennial cropping so that their dependence on swidden cultivation is reduced.

The Forest Department started work in the area made available by the village chief. Some terracing work has been undertaken. Similarly, some afforestation work has been done and in the demonstration plot big cardamom, black pepper, fruit plant and avenue trees have been put up. It does not, however, seem that the tribals are very much impressed by this effort. Our investigations showed that none of the tribals have planted these trees in their own lands. Since cardamom takes three years to fruit, the tribals may not have realized its great possibilities in giving additional income as yet. Other plantations like that of black pepper, tea, and fruit trees have not attracted much attention. May be it is yet too early to expect a marked impact on the tribals. However, the experiment needs to be watched closely. There is a need for greater stress on the extension aspect of the programme. It would be better if the Forest Department concentrates in a few areas over a longer period of time rather than dissipating its energy in replicating the experiment in many more areas. The tribals' interest in the programme up till now is confined to its employment potential rather than in its possibilities to wean them away from swiddening.

Case Study of Resettlement Programme Among the Digaru Mishmi

The Digaru are one of the branches of the Mishmi tribe which is spread over large parts of the Lohit District in Arunachal Pradesh. They are among the second wave of emigrants from Burma who came a little over 500 years ago. Their language bears close affinity to that of Kachins and Chins of Burma. The Digaru are divided into a number of clans and sub-clans. They are rather short-statured and have very pronounced Mongoloid features.

They live in long houses scattered over wide areas. The distance between two houses may be as much as half a mile. Sometimes a village might consist of solitary long house, thus by itself forming a unit. The houses are often very long and large. A rich man's house may be 100 feet long and 15 or more feet broad. A passage runs from one end of the house to the other with a number of small compartments opening into the corridor. Living in long houses has led to the lack of strong social cohesion in the community. The village is not much of a social unit. A village of more than a dozen houses is rare, and some villages have only one or two long houses. Thus the real social unit is the long house.

The Mishmis are all agriculturists now but they practise the most primitive type of agriculture. This is more so because they live in an area which does not have much fertility. Unlike the Wancho area, there is some idea of individual or family property among the Digaru Mishmis. A household may own land within the territorial boundary of the village or the clan. It has been recorded by early scholars that there is not much distinction between private land and clan land. This is attributed to the fact that the households belonging to the same clan and the same village descended from a common ancestor not very far back. As long as a man continues to use the land reclaimed by him, it cannot be taken away from him. Lands closer to a village are often put under permanent cultivation. However, on higher altitudes, swidden cultivation is resorted to.

Unlike the Wancho, the Digaru Mishmi did not have strong political organization. They do not have village chiefs or tribal councils. Men of wealth and wisdom use their influence in keeping peace in the area. It is they who arbitrate in serious cases of dispute. In cases of disputes between two clans, there was no acknowledged mechanism for the administration of justice, and the parties have to resort to self-help.

In swidden cultivation operations, women are more active than men. In fact, men have no work after felling the trees and preparing the *jhum* fields for sowing. From then on menfolk remain idle. It is the women who carry on the different agricultural operations from sowing to harvesting. It is they who sow the seeds with the help of the digging stick. They occasionally use the hoe. Men only guard the crops when they are ready. Since women provide labour, there is premium on polygyny. Idleness and extensive use of opium has sapped the strength of men and made them indolent.

In this state of affairs, it was not possible to administer them effectively and the fruits of development could not be made available to them. It was, therefore, thought necessary that they should be brought to the foot-hills and re-located in sizeable villages so that the administration could take steps for their social, economic and educational development. This was, of course, a long and difficult process since it was not merely the replacement of the mode of production but it also involved a change in the life style and value system of the people. It is gratifying to note that the entire process has worked out smoothly and the people did not experience any serious problems of adjustment. This was on account of careful planning and efficient implementation of resettlement work by well-defined stages and through the help of indigenous leaders. In this task, the administrators, politicians, and social workers worked hand in hand.

In 1972, a detailed survey of some of the villages situated just above the foot-hills about 10 kms. from the district headquarters was taken up. This led to the formulation of the resettlement project. It was decided to bring together people living in seven traditional villages, viz., Tayengku, Duraliang, Tafrogam, Jogam, Bothaliang, Khorailiang and Tajuligam. In the year 1973, development workers used to visit these villages and impressed upon their leaders the desirability of settling in one village on the plains. They were also told that the new settlement would entirely be made by them. The Government would provide them all possible help. One advantage which the people perceived in having a resettlement colony close to their traditional villages was that they were not required to break off their links with these villages all at once. The people of these villages agreed to take advantage of the Government offer. By slow degrees, the people of different villages began to work for the Government on daily wages to reclaim about 1,200 acres of land on both sides of the road. The reclaimed area included the land meant for housing.

In these entire operations, the Deputy Commissioner of Lohit district worked in close collaboration with Shri Soben Tayeng, the then Counsellor and now Member of the *Lok Sabha* (Parliament) and Shri Bamtingso Tayeng, Socio-Cultural Organiser. Both of them belong to the Tayenku village. The government of Arunachal Pradesh allotted fund to the Agriculture Department for the resettlement colony. The new colony came to be known as Tafrogam after the name of one of the traditional villages from which the new settlers came.

In the local dialect *Tafra* means undulating surface and *Gam* means village. As a matter of fact, the old village of Tafrogam was situated on a nearby hill slope and correctly conveyed the local meaning. The present site of the new settlement is, however, quite plain and ideally suited for settled cultivation. When the project began, this area was full of thick jungles and large herds of elephants were seen at that place. Although the building of the new settlement was the responsibility of the Agriculture Department, the general administration and local leaders did lend their hand. Among the staff of the Agriculture Department who were sincerely devoted to the task, mention may be made of the Village Level Worker and the Surveyor. The Deputy Commissioner himself took keen interest in the resettlement programme and saw to it that administrative delays were reduced to the minimum.

Since all the land was cleared for agriculture by the people themselves, they felt strong attachment to the new settlement. The allotment of land was controlled by the Government. Each head of household was allowed to take a minimum of two acres and a maximum of thirty acres according to the size of the family and the working capacity of the members of the household. For clearing the jungle they were paid at the rate of Rs.200/- per acre. The big timber trees were sold by auction by the Forest Department. When the work began, the tribals used to come down from the hills to clear the jungle and go back to their houses. Some staff of the Agriculture Department stayed at the village site for survey and looking after the demonstration plots. Gradually, the tribals got acquainted with the methods of settled cultivation. At first, only dry crops were taken up. In course of time, a streamlet at a distance of 7 kms. from the village was dammed and pipelines were laid to make irrigation water available to the new settlement. Soon, almost all the families from the seven villages came down to the new settlement and built their houses themselves in the traditional pattern. Each family was paid a sum of Rs.2000/- for the construction of the house. However, this was not sufficient and most of them had to spend another thousand rupees for building a house according to their needs and liking. Residential plots were allotted according to the plan. Houses were built on both sides of the street which were later on connected with all weather road with district headquarters at Teju. The new settlement was inaugurated by the Lieutenant Governor, in 1975.

By 1979, the water supply scheme was completed. 8" pipes were laid for the purposes of irrigation. Thus, plots which were not far from the pipe-line were given water for wet-rice cultivation. As wet-rice cultivation involves complex procedures, Agriculture Department staff demonstrated all the processes from seed preparation, field ploughing and transplantation up to harvesting and threshing. The Village Level Worker went from door to door to involve people and train them in the use of the new techniques.

Now some of the households in the village practise wet-rice cultivation along with dry crops. Even high yielding varieties are being used by the tribals. The Agriculture Department supplies fertilizers at 75 per cent subsidy and seeds at 50 per cent subsidy. For the purchase of bullocks, 50 per cent subsidy is given. However, only a few cultivators have purchased bullocks, as the departmental tractor is lent to the tribals for ploughing. The people of Tafrogam do not employ labourers from outside or rent out their lands for wet-rice cultivation. The Agriculture Department supplies all the requirements of tools and implements. It also provides periodical training in plant protection and other techniques. For this purpose, instructors from the Farmers' Training School at Kherem come. When the cultivators are sent for training anywhere else, they are paid a sum of Rs.10/- per day. In addition to the settled cultivation, most of the new settlers sometimes go to their traditional villages and collect whatever produce they can from their old plots. They have not as yet given up their claims on their earlier holdings.

It is interesting and useful to study the impact of the change on the life of the people. It may be mentioned that the new settlers came from villages which were not situated on a very high altitude. All the seven traditional villages were situated at an elevation of between 2000 to 3000 feet. Due to the growth of population, the *Jhum* cycle has been reduced to 5 to 7 years. They were also experiencing difficulty on account of low yield from the land. On the hills, they used to grow marua, maize, kochu, sweet potato, tapioca, chillies, and coarse rice. Among the vegetables, they produced potatoes, brinjals, *bhindi* (okra), *kaddu* (gourd), *kohra* (gourd). In addition, they produced some quantities of mustard, turmeric and ginger. By the use of the new agricultural technology, the tribals have seen that it is possible to produce much more grain per acre. The average quantity of grain produced by the *Jhum* method was 3/4 quintals per acre. Now with settled cultivation people are able to get 5 to 8 quintals per acre from the dry rice cultivation and 8 to 10 quintals per acre from the wet-rice cultivation. By using the high yielding varieties of seed, some tribals have also got 15 quintals of paddy per acre. The enhanced yield has lifted them above the subsistence level. In addition to rice, they are now producing some cash crops like mustard and ginger. They are also producing large quantities of fruits such as orange, pineapple, and banana. They have taken up the cultivation of maize, millet, sweet potato, pulses like *arhar*, moong etc, sugarcane, sesamum, onion, garlic, green peas, and even wheat. The District Agriculture Officer collects all the cash crops and sends it to Tinsukia by a departmental vehicle for sale. The department charges at the rate of Rs.11/- per quintal as freight. Some of the villagers also go on the vehicle and sell the cash crops at maximum price. In 1982, the produce of the sale of mustard from this area was as high as Rs.200,000. The fruits grown in their village are sold in the neighbouring district town.

The bulk of the people in Tafrogam are not able to take advantage of wet-rice cultivation because of the insufficient supply of water for irrigation. To remove this difficulty, the Central P.W.D. is shortly laying 24" pipeline from a nearby Micro-hydel project. However, even dry paddy cultivation has led to a general improvement in the standard of living. The surplus paddy is either sold in the market or given as loan to people from the interior hill villages.

The Mishmi are very lavish in spending on celebrations of different rites and rituals including those of birth, marriage and death. On each occasion, they give feasts to their kinsfolk for which *mithuns* (Bos Frontalis), pigs and fowls are killed. A good quantity of rice is also used for making rice beer.

Despite the socio-cultural constraints detailed above, settled cultivation has bestowed upon the people a new quality of life and their level of aspirations has gone up. Exposure to outside influences, the impact of education and nearness of district headquarters have opened new opportunities for them. 20 per cent of the households get a surplus from their agricultural produce. Besides these, a number of people from the village are in Government employment. There are 12 employees in the grade IV and 3 in grade III. Some of them continue to live in the village while others visit the village off and on to supplement the income of the family. The new agricultural technology has made it possible for them to grow high yielding varieties of such crops as paddy, wheat, maize, potato, pulses, oilseeds and sugarcane. In the year 1982-1983, ten acres were used for growing orange and 17 acres for growing pineapple.

The consumption of chemical fertilizers has also grown over the years.

One cultivator raised a crop of 35 quintals in 3 acres in wet-rice cultivation. In 1981, besides getting 40 quintals of paddy in the irrigated patch of 3 acres, he gathered a harvest of 12 quintals of wheat, 9 quintals of mustard, and 15 quintals of paddy through dry cultivation. In 1982, he got 35 quintals through wet-rice cultivation and 10 quintals of mustard and 10 quintals of potato through dry cultivation.

The government has concentrated a large number of developmental activities in this village. There are pig, goat, and dairy farms in the village. People are encouraged to get loans to start such farms from the State Bank of India. In each house, beneath platforms used as floor, pigs and poultry are kept in separate enclosures. These are looked after by women, and are treated as women's wealth. However, the improved breed of poultry could not survive and the poultry farm has now been deserted. This is on account of the fact that no staff was provided to look after the farm and the birds died on account of wrong feed which caused a disease. The local breed is immune to that disease. Improved pigs could be seen in each house. Piglings are available on 50 per cent subsidy basis from the pig farm in the village. There are arrangements for cross-breeding the local breed with the improved breed. Formerly, the tribesmen did not take any milk. Now villagers and government staff living in the village are supplied milk from a dairy maintained by the government. Since milk is now readily available and the tribals can afford to buy it, it is used in most of the households. Arrangement has been made to provide one hydrant for each house.

People in this village have been quite enthusiastic about education. It seems that even while living in the traditional villages they had craving for education with the result that the village can now boast of two college graduates, two higher secondary graduates, and 4 matriculates. 15 students from the village are in the hostel of the Higher Secondary School at Tezu. The village has a pre-primary as well as a primary school. The pre-primary school was established in 1982. Out of a total enrolment of 18, two thirds are boys and the rest are girls. In the primary school, the total enrolment is 65 out of whom 52 are tribals. Among the tribals, there are 39 boys and 13 girls. It is seen that after Class III, the number of tribal pupils begins to fall. There are 7 girls from this village in the Vivekanand Girls Middle School which is located at a distance of 3 kms. on the hills. There are 6 students from this village in the Vivekanand Kendriya Vidyalaya at Sonpura. There is also one student in the Special Central School in Delhi.

In the new village, there are people from various clans. Out of the 85 households, 47 belong to the Tayeng Clan and 7 to Beli. Other clans are Doo, Moro, Tunda, Sai, Siba, Thale, etc. None of these has more than 5 members each. The total population is 508; the average family size is 6. The size of the holding differs from 3 acres to 37 acres of dry land. 11 families have more than 10 acres of dry land. At present, 19 families practise wet-rice cultivation in addition to dry cultivation. The wet holdings range between 2 to 5 acres. The total land available for rice cultivation is 52 acres. This is likely to go up when irrigation water from the 24" pipeline is made available. Only 19 families keep domestic cattle. The total number of cattle in the village is 46. As mentioned earlier, the main credit for the coming up of the resettlement colony and its growth on the right lines goes to two leaders, Mr. Sobeng Tayeng and Mr. Bramtingso Tayeng. It is to them that the settlers always looked up for advice and guidance in all matters. Sobeng Tayeng has been one such leader. He was born in 1941 and passed the Matriculation examination from Tezu High School in 1963. He passed his B.A. from Benaras Hindu University in 1967. He was a member of Social Advisory Board of NEFA and also Vice-president of All Arunachal Pradesh Student Union. From 1967 to 1969, he was employed in the Planning Department in NEFA Secretariat for ten months in 1971. In 1972 he was appointed Councillor-in-charge of Forest Industry and Co-operation. When Arunachal Pradesh became a state in 1975, he became Minister for Forest, Industry and Agriculture. He continued as Minister for four years. Now, he is a Congress (I) M.P. He has a large modern looking house in Tafrogam.

The other leader is Bramtingso Tayeng. He was also born in 1941. He was educated in Tezu. In 1957-1958, he was deputed to the Teacher's Training Institute at Margherita for Hindi Teacher's Training Course. Thereafter, he was appointed a primary school teacher in the Lohit district. He also opened five new L.P. Schools. From 1965-1972, he worked as Local Dialect Translator for the

Digaru Mishmi dialect. In 1973, he was appointed Social and Cultural Organiser and is still serving in that capacity. In 1962, he was awarded a silver medal by the Governor of Assam for meritorious service. In 1975-1976, he was awarded a second silver medal. He is keenly interested in agricultural development and is closely connected with all social institutions and local affairs. He is very forward looking and is widely travelled. He is able to devote the bulk of his time for development of his own village.

Looking back at this case of a successful attempt at resettlement of a tribal community, we are in a position to answer some of the questions that are usually raised on this issue. In this particular case, the people of the seven traditional villages were not entirely isolated, they were exposed to outside influences on account of some of their own members who had gone out for employment or for education. Thus, they did not offer any resistence to moving down the hills provided they were given land, housing, and other facilities by the government. They had also the advantage of receiving guidance from the two local leaders mentioned above. In addition to this their minds were constantly prepared for change by visits and discussions with government officers. The people had known the advantages of settled cultivation and they chose the new alternative. This shows that all people have an inner urge to better their quality of life. In fact, the poor have no compulsion to stay poor. Swiddening only provided them with bare subsistence. On the other hand, settled cultivation held promises of a surplus which could be used for improvement of their standard of living and also for meeting their kinship obligations in a better way.

The people who moved out did not completely sever their links with their old villages. They still go there for hunting and to collect whatever produce they can from the *jhum* fields. All the people from these villages moved to the new settlement. None was left behind. Each head of the household was anxious to take maximum advantage from the new opportunity.

Social anthropologists have often asserted that the tribals are very devoted to the deities and rituals and on account of these they are bound to the hills. It is true that swiddening is not merely an agricultural practice but a way of life. The change from swiddening to settled cultivation involves a change in the nature of ownership of land. In the Digaru Mishmi area, however, tribals had some notion of private property and land and, therefore, it was not advantageous for them to get land registered in their own names in the new settlement. The religious rituals still continue to be performed as of old. None of their festivals seem to have been connected with the swiddening calendar.

The change seems to have affected the role of women. It has been observed above that the entire agricultural operations after the preparation of the ground for sowing are carried on by women. In settled cultivation, however, with the use of the plough or the tractor, women have a reduced role in agriculture. It is now possible for them to give more time to the rearing of pigs, poultry and goats. It has given them some more leisure than before, The work-load of men has certainly increased. They have not only to look after agricultural operations, but also to manage the sale of their surplus of agricultural produce. They have to give some more time for learning the new techniques of agriculture. They are also busy with managing their own affairs with the help of the new *Panchayat* (village council) for which an election was held in September 1983. In this election, 8 persons have been elected as members of *Gram Panchayat,* 5 of them belonging to the Tayeng clan and 3 belonging to the minor clans in the village. One of these members has also become a Member of the *Anchal Panchayat.*

Since there was no system of hereditary chiefs in this community, the democratic system of elections has been welcomed by them. The face of the Leadership is turned towards change. They are taking advantage of the subsidy made available to them through the Intensive Rural Development Programme (IRDP). They have received loans from the State Bank of India for the purchase of seeds and implements. They seem to be anxious for attaining a higher standard of living. Some of the villagers have also taken to petty business like running flour-mills, and contract work. Two ultra modern houses have come up and the third one is half complete. The people are satisfied that they have themselves opted for settled cultivation which held promises of a better future. They are happy that by their own labour and through the help of the government, they have achieved their desired goal. They, however, are anxious for further improvement. They feel that the school needs expansion and that better drinking water facilities should be available.

Outlook for the Future and Theoretical Implications

This study was undertaken to view the problem of swidden cultivation from the twin perspective of culture and environment. Faced by the problem of development and anxious to better the quality of life, administrators and planners tend to overlook the cultural imperatives. Communities, on the other hand, confronted by hunger tend to destroy the forests in the absence of any other satisfactory means of making a living. Sometimes too much concern with the environment may lead to complete neglect of a people's culture. However, culture itself cannot survive unless people can cope with problems of environmental degradation.

An attempt has been made in this study not only to look at both the aspects of the problem but also try to find out how people themselves view the situation. It may be said that swidden cultivation is not a practice peculiar only to the primitive tribes. Evidence from Sri Lanka, Thailand, and Republic of Korea seems to contradict this stereotype. In Sri Lanka it is practised by the Sinhala speaking people. In the Republic of Korea, in the northern most part, it is practised by those people who escape to the mountains for political, economic and religious reasons. In Thailand, swiddeners have been largely identified with opium cultivators. Similarly, in Arunachal Pradesh, the practice is widespread on account of the non-availability of land for settled cultivation. Traditional swidden cultivators like the Nishi carry on wet-rice cultivation in small patches in narrow valleys. Given plain land along with agricultural inputs, the Digaru Mishmi have, in course of 5 years, been converted into the settled cultivators. Thus, swiddening is not a synonym for backwardness either agricultural or cultural.

Swidden cultivation cannot be viewed as only an economic activity since all economic relations are set in a social framework. Each case of swiddening has to be studied in its specific historical, physiographic, and socio-political context. Swiddening among the Wancho is closely integrated with their political and social systems. The chief holds absolute power over land communally owned; and he distributes land to heads of households according to their needs as well as their capacity to cultivate the land. Since no private ownership of land is acknowledged, there is no incentive among the people to develop the land. Endemic wars and raids in the past increased the power of the chief. If people had to supplement their income, it was only through working as casual daily labourers either in road construction work or in forest plantations. Their social system too was inextricably woven with the politico-economic structure.

We did not find swidden cultivation to be uneconomical. It could be so had other alternatives been available. In the Wancho case, people had no choice. Swiddening is the only possible way left to them to get subsistence. And it is hard to say that their practice has destroyed the environment. The area in which the Wancho practise swiddening is very open; therefore, the question of pollution of the air does not occur. On account of the long period of fallow, vegetation comes up. The Wancho did not destroy the roots of big trees, and therefore these regenerate in no time. To check soil erosion and the formation of gullies by fast flow of the water down hill, sometimes logs of wood are placed on the slopes and it is seen that the furrows are horizontal and not vertical. People are aware of the dangers of soil erosion and they see to it that it is reduced to the minimum.

Since swidden cultivation cannot be stopped by constant condemnation, it is imperative to think of a positive policy towards it. We have, therefore, to think of scientific swiddening. On the basis of empirical knowledge gained by the people themselves through centuries and knowledge gained through researches on high altitude cultivation, improvements ought to be introduced. In any situation of man-environment interaction, some exploitation is always implied. Therefore, some damage to the environment is inevitable no matter what form of agriculture people practise. Some form of environmental exploitation is always needed for the survival of people.

Swiddening has been differently perceived by academic experts, administrators and people. Some agricultural experts feel that it is very wasteful system of land use as it leads to continuous depletion of scarce forest resources, affects rainfall, causes washing down of the sub-soil, leads to floods and generally adversely affects the environment. However, some other experts hold that this form of cultivation is the most pragmatic approach to the ecological compulsions of a given region. It may be the only possible method of land use in a particular area. This is also the view of the bulk of the people practising swidden cultivation among the Wancho.

Government officials, on the other hand, are intrigued by the practice as it creates special difficulties for them in bringing education, health and other social services to the scattered population. Forest officials look at it as an unmitigated evil. They regard that the tribals are destroying forests with a vengeance. Forests are essential not only for the present generation but for the coming generations as well. If the forests are gone, not only will the environment be poorer but the climate would change and there will be a great deal of suffering. However, the alternative that they suggest for the people who have hitherto practised swiddening involves a change in work habits, patterns of ownership, and established processes of political control and decision making.

Our own view is that the correct approach to the problem of swidden cultivation lies in accepting it not as a "necessary evil", but in recognising it as a "way of life". It should not be condemned as an evil practice but regarded as a technique evolved by the people in their effort to meet the challenges of the difficult physiography. For a long time, the practice has been condemned as a case to be ashamed of and as a kind of vandalism that has to be stopped at all costs. This attitude breeds inferiority complex and unhealthy atmosphere for launching the so-called development schemes to control or stop swiddening. Since the whole life of the people revolves round swiddening throughout the area, there is intermeshing between economy and culture. Any step, therefore, to deal with the situation should be based on a detailed study of the agricultural methods and the social implications of *jhuming*. Any programme of agricultural reform based on the total stoppage of the time-honoured system is likely to lead to a breakdown of their norms resulting in a societal crisis. Swiddening is a form of co-operative, communal farming while permanent cultivation like wet-rice cultivation turned people towards private ownership. This in itself would lead to a disturbance of old traditions.

Mahapatra (1979:9) proposed a four fold classification of swidden cultivation. The Wancho present an instance of the first type i.e. those who subsist by exclusive dependence. In this no other type of cultivation is practised since the land for settled cultivation is just not available. The technology is very simple and division of labour is based only on age and sex. For the Wancho, swidden is the only method of cultivation as it is adapted to their topography, climate, and manpower resources. Land is owned by the village. It is apportioned by the chief of heads of households according to the manpower available with them. The capital investment is minimal. The only labour available is the household manpower. A large variety of crops are grown including rice, millets, pulses, vegetables, and fruits. There is no risk of total crop failure. As the crops ripen at different times of the year some food supply is assured round the year.

It is seen that Wancho children from the age of eleven start their life as swidden cultivators. They have inherited this system from their forefathers. They did not know any alternative technique. Most of the people do not think that this system is bad, nor are they aware of its evils. Tradition ordains that full-grown trees are not to be uprooted. Only the big branches are lopped off. Sometimes big logs are placed at different levels to prevent soil from being washed down. In addition to this the *jhum* cycle is still 10 to 11 years during which time the different plots recuperate their fertility and the forests are regenerated. The swiddeners also dislike the idea of being resettled somewhere else. They are in favour of *in-situ* development. The total population in the area is still small, even though the density of population among the Wancho is among the highest in Arunachal Pradesh. Even the village leaders do not regard swiddening as bad for the environment. They are, however, in favour of better farming methods. Members of the *Anchal Samiti* however, realized that swiddening causes soil erosion. They also realize that in swiddening the yield is lower than in permanent cultivation. However, with some fertilizer input, the produce per acre of swidden does not compare very unfavourably with the produce in the wet cultivated areas. It is interesting to find that the *Anchal Samiti* members thought that the swiddeners might go in for alternative sources of income. Two of their worst problems are communication and illiteracy. The *Samiti* members are indeed forward looking and they are not generally attached too much to their customary practices. The development officers, on the other hand, in a large measure, think that swidden cultivation is bad for the environment as it causes soil erosion and its yields are lower than those in permanent cultivation.

It would be useful to have a look at the economics of swidden cultivation. It has been indicated by Saha (1970) that this system of cultivation can maintain at least 18 to 22 persons per sq. km. The density of population in the Wancho area is only 12 at present. So, for few decades swidden cultivation can continue in the area. However, it leaves little surplus for upliftment of the people in the area. It has very little scope for specialization as diverse crops are sown in a single plot of land. Even if some surplus is generated by some households, the scope for investment in agriculture is limited. Improved agricultural tools and implements and the desire to invest in agriculture is hemmed by lack of opportunity. Improved agricultural tools and instruments and seeds suitable for these areas are yet to be evolved. Since there is no suitable avenue for investment, the surplus wealth of some affluent farmers is diverted to procure more wives, more *mithuns,* ornaments, opium, guns and transistors. It has been noted above that swiddening is associated with traditional communal ownership of land. Whatever right the household has on its plot of land is suspended as soon as its members stop cultivation. As such swiddening provides hardly any motivation to the cultivators. It is based on low technology and under utilization of human resources. Mostly primitive tools are used. In the Wancho area the ripe grain is picked up by hand. The sickle is largely unknown. It is pointed out that swidden cultivation by itself fails to provide food to the farmers who have to supplement their earning by hunting and food gathering and also by full-time employment as casual labourers.

Any attempt to solve this problem has to be two dimensional. The first relates to adoption of methods designed to curtail it and second, to eliminate its harmful effects. Both these aspects may differ from area to area and therefore, no generalization may be advanced. There is, however unanimity on the question of encouraging scientific swidden cultivation. For instance, the cut tree-trunks may be placed across the slopes to reduce the velocity of running water. This will prevent soil erosion to a large extent. Secondly, the cultivators may be advised to make furrows across the slope rather than along it. This will also counter soil erosion and would help the retention of moisture. Thirdly, the planting of leguminous and other crops may have immediate effect of regenerating vegetation and binding the soil. In areas where the slope is not very steep, terraces can be made. Along with this, horticulture may be encouraged and cultivators be urged to adopt afforestation scheme. Many cash crops like cardamom, black pepper, coffee plants etc. have at least a three year gestation period. Pineapple, orange, and banana plantation may also be promoted in these areas. However ultimately, the marketing of these products will have to be made by state sponsored organisations. Communication difficulties are a big depressant. These efforts may be supplemented by livestock and poultry farming. In suitable areas, bee keeping and silk worm rearing may also be encouraged.

The efforts made by the Forest Department to control swiddening through some of their schemes had not been very successful. The cardamom, pepper and coffee plantation in some of the villages are looked upon by the tribals as an avenue of employment as casual labourers of the Forest Department. The plantations are on the lands given by the village chief. None of these plantations are, therefore, regarded as the property of any household and therefore, no personal interest is involved. This can only be done if there is some change in the ownership of land. This at the present time seems unlikely. The other difficulty is about three year gestation period during which the food requirements of the households are to be met.

Our experience in the Digaru Mishmi area in the neighbouring district of Lohit has been very encouraging. There, the situation has been somewhat different. This tribe lived on the lower slopes and could easily move down to the foot-hills, as soon as the government resettlement colony came to be established. Here land was available and private ownership was given to individual families. In course of time, the tribals made the plain land cultivable. House-sites and building subsidies were also given to them. Infrastructural facilities were also made available. They had the advantage of enlightened leadership. They were also very close to the district headquarters which ensured continued presence and supervision of district level development officials. The tribals took advantage of the situation. Though attached to the practice of swidden cultivation, they gave it up because the alternative was more tempting.

This research exercise yielded valuable dividends in terms of theoretical insights which are listed below:

1. Swiddening has become a problem since the concerns of the wider society are impinging on the life of people living in little communities. Hitherto these little communities have been largely isolated from the larger populations. With the development of communications and the consequent process of integration of the little communities with the wider society, it is no longer possible for people in the

simpler societies to carry on their activities in a way as if they existed in a closed society. In the areas where swiddening is done there are enormous forest resources. These resources are no longer considered the preserve of the communities who live nearby. They are regarded as the wealth of the state and as such the latter sees to it that they do not want only to be destroyed. If no steps are taken, in a few generations, all the forests would disappear leading to adverse climatic consequences. However, in order to protect the forest, it is not necessary to ban swiddening altogether. Effective steps need be taken to strike a balance between the claims of the wider society and the interests of the little communities.

2. It is argued that in primitive societies, the prime determinants of behaviour are social rather than economic. However, the primacy of social factors has not been explicitly argued in relation to the determination of production and resource allocation in primitive societies. Anthropologists concede that economic variables are important and they do take notice of economic, ecological, and technological data. However, in a dynamic society, it seems that economic rationality has been separated from cultural considerations. This has largely been made possible by the introduction of cash crops. Food provides only subsistence but cash takes care of much more and it is a valuable lever to raise the standard of living. If people take to cash crops it may be a big motivation to give up swiddening.

3. There is a need to find a middle range view somewhere between the environmental and cultural determinism. It has been shown that wherever a satisfactory alternative has been provided, cultural considerations do not pose an insuperable barrier to change. This has been seen in the case of the Digaru Mishmi. It has been seen in the two villages of Zedua and Rusa in the Wancho area where some plain land is available for wet-rice cultivation. In both these villages some Wancho people have taken to the new method of rice production. The bulk of the people in the Wancho area are not taking to select cultivation since the alternatives are not available and those that are available in the form of swidden cultivation control measures are not satisfactory because of the long gestation period of the cash crops and the absence of private ownership in land.

4. It must be noted that wherever some agriculture is carried on there is some exploitation of the environment resulting in degradation

of the soil. It may be argued that on account of the thin coverage of soil on the hills, erosion may be faster, and the degradation may be quicker and total. However, suitable steps may be devised to arrest the process of soil erosion by introducing such crops that hold the soil in a better way. Some relief may also be provided to people through reduction of the pressure on land by the introduction of well designed programmes of animal husbandry.

5. It is necessary to probe deeper into the conditions that promote swiddening and allow it to persist in different areas. Since conditions differ from area to area a different mix of steps may be necessary to deal with the situation.

6. We may also have to decide that if we condemn swiddening at all, do we condemn all its different varieties or only some kinds of it? This is essential because the harm ultimately done to the ecology in each variety is different.

At the end of study, we are in a position to make suggestions for further work in this area. In the limited perspective which we adopted for this study it was not possible to cover all aspects of the problem. Later researchers might take them up according to their interest and resources.

1. The *emic* perspective of the quality of environment and the quality of life should be worked out in greater detail. The quality of the environment should be examined in terms of the value system of swiddeners. This will throw some light on the debate whether they should retain their ways or should we change them to our ways. If they are to change, should they bring about the change themselves? We have to know what they want. We should also know as to who determines the direction in which they would move.

2. What happens to the cultural norms of the swiddeners when they take up to permanent cultivation? This is important in view of the fact that their entire life revolves round the practice of swiddening.

3. A change in the agricultural practice leads to a change in the relationship between man and land. The agriculturist is bound to his land by spiritual and religious ties. In course of time, with permanent cultivation, land might become only an economic asset completely devoid of any religious or spiritual substance.

4. It would be necessary to examine, in this context, the internal dynamics in each society and analyse if internal forces can themselves promote evolutionary changes.

5. There should be an inventory of swiddening techniques among ethnic groups working in different environments. This knowledge can provide solutions or spread knowledge to countries where swiddening is still practised. This would generate ideas on improving swiddening rather than replacing it with permanent cultivation. This seems necessary as modern agronomy does not pay attention to improving swiddening.

6. In areas where there is a shortage of plain agricultural land, one should examine if the hill slopes can better be utilised for swiddening than allowing it to remain forested

7. The possibility of large scale joint research project which could bring together social and natural scientists for the study of swiddening may be explored.

8. It would be useful to examine the stage at which economic imperatives override cultural norms and where single rationality is replaced by alternative rationality.

SELECT BIBLIOGRAPHY

Baruah,T.K. 1960: *The Idu Mishmi*, Shillong, N.E.F.A. Administration.

Bohidar,N. 1972-73: Problem of shifting cultivation with special reference to Balliguda Division. *Adibasi,* Bhubaneshwar, Vol.XIV., No.4.

Borah, D. and Goswami, N.R. 1977: *A Comparative Study of Crop production under shifting and terrace cultivation* (mimeographed). Jorhat, Agro-Economic Research Centre for North-East India.

Bose, S. 1967: *Carrying capacity of land under shifting cultivation.* Asiatic Society Monograph Series, Vol.XII, Calcutta.

Bose S., Ghatak S. etal.1982 "Shifting Cultivation in India" in K.S Singh, ed., *Economic of the Tribe and their Transformation.* New Delhi: Concept Publishing Company.

Burling, R. 1963: *Rangsanggri Family and Kinship in Garo village.* Philadelphia University Press.

Chandra, R.R. 1970-71: Tribal economy. *Adibasi*, Bhubaneshwar, Vol.XII, No. 1-4

Chatterjee, B.K. 1954: Summary of a Paper presented at *Tribal Welfare Conference* at Lohardaga.

Chaudhary, B. 1967-68: Economic activities of Pauri Bhuiya, *Adibasi*, Bhubaneshwar, Vol. IX, No.3

Chowdhury, J.N. *The Hill Miris of Subansiri*, Shillong, N.E.F.A. Administration. Commissioner for Scheduled Castes and Scheduled Tribes 1955 Report; New Delhi, Government of India

—— 1961: Report; New Delhi, Government of India

—— 1968: Report on Techno-Economic Survey of Nagaland; New Delhi, Government of India.

Conklin, H.C. 1957: *Hanunoo agriculture in the Philippines.* FAO Rome

—— 1961: Study of shifting cultivation. *Current Anthropology*. Chicago, Vol. II, No.I.

Danda, D. 1978: *Among the Dimasa of Assam: an ethnographic Study*. New Delhi, Sterling publications.

Dar, Usha 1970: Shifting cultivation in the hill tracts of India. *Indian Journal of Agricultural Economics*. Bombay, Vol.XXV, No.3.

Das, N.K. 1977: Agrarian structure and change in Nagaland. Paper presented in the "Workshop on Tribal Economy". *Anthropological Survey of India*. Calcutta.

Das, T.C. 1931: *Wild Kharias of Dalbhum*. Calcutta, University of Calcutta.

—— 1945: *The Purum: an old Kuki tribe of Manipur*. Calcutta, University of Calcutta.

Das Gupta, S.B. 1978: *Birjhia: a section of Chotanagpur*. Calcutta, K.P. Bagchi and Company.

Dube, S.C. 1951: *The Kamar*. Lucknow, Universal Publishers.

Dutta, P.C. 1981: "Cultural and Historical Background of the Wanchos of Arunachal Pradesh. "*In North-Eastern Times*, Gauhati, Nov. - Dec.1981.

Dutta Chodhary, S. ed. 1980: *Tirap District Gazetteer*. Shillong: Government of Arunachal Pradesh

Elwin, V. 1939: *The Baigas*. London, John Murray.

—— 1963: A New Deal for Tribal India. New Delhi. Ministry of Home Affairs.

FAO Staff 1957: Shifting cultivation. *The Unasylva*, Vol.XI, Rome.

Fuchs,S. 1960: *The Gonds and Bhumia of Eastern Mandla*. Bombay, Asia Publishers.

Ganguli, J.B. 1969: *Economic problems of Jhumias of Tripura*. Calcutta, Bookland.

—— 1976 *Socio-economic problems of transition from shifting to sedentary cultivation in North-East India*. North East India Council for Social Science Research.

Gohain, B.C. 1953: Shifting cultivation among the Abors. *The March of India*, Vol. VI. No.2.

Gohain, D. 1977: *Apple cultivation in Arunachal Pradesh: A study in Kameng District* (mimeographed). Jorhat, Agro-Economic Research Centre.

Goswami, P.C. 1968: *Shifting cultivation and its control in Garo Hills*. Assam, Social Conservation Department.

—— 1969: *Economic problems of Jhumias of Tripura*. Calcutta.

Bookland.

Goswami, P.C. and Saikia, P.D. 1970: Problem of agricultural development in Tribal Areas. *Indian Journal of Agricultural Economics*. Bombay, Vol. XXXIII, No.4.

Grigson, W.G. 1938: *The Maria Gonds of Bastar*. Oxford University Press.

Gupta, T. and Sambrani, S.K. 1978: Farming system in Hill areas. *Indian Journal of Agricultural Economics*, Bombay, Vol.XXV, No.4.

Haimendorf, C. Von. Furer. 1945: *Tribal Hyderabad*. Hyderabad, Revenue Department.

—— 1945: The Reddis of the Bison Hills, Macmillan & Co., London.

—— 1962: *The Apatanis and their Neighbours*, London, Routledge and Kegan Paul

—— 1979: *The Gonds of Andhra Pradesh*, New Delhi, Vikas

Hodson, T.C. 1974: *The Naga Tribes of Manipur*. Delhi, B.R. Publishing Corporation.

Hungyo, P. 1977: The economic life of the Tangkhul Nagars, with special reference to shifting cultivation. Paper presented in the *Workshop on Tribal Economy*. Anthropological Survey of India. Calcutta.

Hutton, J.H. 1968: *The Sema Nagas*. Oxford University Press.

—— 1969: *The Angami Nagas*. Oxford University Press.

Jay, Edward J. 1970: *A tribal village of middle India*. Calcutta, Anthropological Survey of India.

—— 1974: A comparison of tribal and peasant villages in India. *Journal of the Indian Anthropological society*, Vol.IX, No.I.

Kabiraj, S. 1962: Jhum cultivation of the Garos and Rain, *Folklore*, Vol.III,No.12.

Kaith, D.C. 1958: *Shifting cultivation practices in India*. New Delhi, I.C.A.R.

Kaul, S.K. 1976: Human aspects of forest development in North-East India. *Tribe*, Udaipur, Vol. IX,NO.4.

Mahapatra, L.K. 1953: Summary of Papers on *Tribal Welfare Conference*, at Lohardaga.

—— 1965: From shifting cultivator to agriculturist - the Pauri Bhuiyan in transition.
Adibasi, Bhubaneshwar, Vol.VII, No. 2.

—— 1979: Country statement: India, a comparative study on swidden cultivation in Asia; *Report of a Unesco Regional Meeting of Ex-*

perts, Bangkok.

Mahapatra, K. and Devi Kiranbala 1972-73: Shifting cultivation in Orissa. *Adibasi*, Bhubancshwar, Vol. XIV, No.4.

Mahapatra, P.K. 1969-70: Handbook on Koya. *Adibasi*, Bhubaneshwar, Vol.XI,No.4.

—— 1976: *Political organization and social change in a tribe in Orissa*. Ph.D. Thesis submitted to Ranshi University (unpublished).

Mandal, Debabrata 1977: Some aspects of the economy of the Pengos of Karaput District Orissa. Paper presented in the *Workshop on Tribal Economy*, Anthropological Survey of India. Calcutta.

Mathur, K.S. 1976: Human aspects of forest development in North-East India. *Tribe*, Udaipur, Vol.IX, No.4.

Mazumdar, D.N. 1966: *The Garos*. Gauhati, Lawyers Book Stall.

Mills, J.P. 1926: *The Ao Nagas*. London, MacMillan.

Mishra, P.K. 1970: Economic development among the Jenukurubas. *Man in India*, Ranch, Vol. 50. No.1.

Morab, S.G. 1977: Shifting cultivation among the Hill Soliga. Paper presented in the *Workshop in Tribal Economy*. Anthropological Survey of India. Calcutta.

Mukherjee, R.K 1975: Some social constraints to agricultural development in North-East India. *North-Eastern Affairs*, Annual Issue.

Nag, D.S. 1958: *Tribal economy: an economic study of the Baiga*. Delhi, Bhartiya Adimjati Sevak Sangh.

Pal, B.N. 1980: "Some economic aspects of tribal agriculture". In Vidyarthi and Sahay: *Applied Anothropology and development in India*. New Delhi, National Publishing House.

Patel, M.L. 1968: Social dimensions of forest development policy of Madhya Pradesh. *Vanyajati* Vol. IV, No. 2.

Patnaik,N. 1977: Shifting cultivation in Orissa, *Adibasi*, Vol. XVI, No. 4.

Perry, N.E. 1932: The Lakhers. London, Macmillan.

Prasad, S. 1971: Kurwa: the shifting cultivation of the Maler. *Vanyajati*, New Delhi, Vol.XIX, No.2.

Raju, Mvt. 1971: A study of tribal rehabilitation programme in Jatapu, Kotapadu Colony, Srikakulam, Andhra Pradesh. *Journal of the Indian Anthropological Society,* Vol. VI, No. 1.

Robinson, H.R 1972: *Monsoon Asia*, London, Macdonald & Evans Ltd.

Rout, S.P 1969: Hand book on the Juang. *Adibasi,* Bhubaneshwar,

Vol.XI, No.1-2.

Roy Burman, B.K. 1960: *Dynamics of persistence and change of small community* -
Ph.D. dissertation, Calcutta University (unpublished).

—— 1966: Monograph on Warmung - an Ao Naga village in Nagaland-*Census of India*, Vol. I, Part VI., New Delhi, office of the Registrar - General of India.

—— 1961: Demographic and socio-economic profile of the Hill Areas of North-East India, *Census of India,* New Delhi.

Roy Burman, B.K and Sharma, P.S. 1970: Dominant mode of agriculture among the Tribals. *Indian Journal of Agricultural Economics*, Bombay, Vol. XXV, No.3.

Ramakrishnan, P.S. Toky, O.P. et al. 1978: "Slash and Burn Cultivation in North-Eastern India." *Proceedings of the Conference on Fire Regimes and Eco-System Properties*. Honolulu, Hawaii.

Sachchidananda, Pathak, K.N. 1983: "India" in *Swidden Cultivation in Asia*, Vol.II, Bangkok: Unesco, pp.I-107.

Saikia, P.D. and Kalita Chitra 1979: *Agricultural production, land and labour utilization in Hill Areas of North-East India* (mimeographed), Jorhat, Agro-Economic Research Centre.

Saikia, P.D. 1982: " A Note on shifting Cultivation in North-Eastern India." In K.S Singh, ed., *Economic of the Tribes and Their Transformation*. New Delhi: Concept Publishing Company.

Srivastava, L.R.N 1973: *Among the Wanchos of Arunachal Pradesh*. Research Department, Shillong: Arunachal Pradesh Administration.

Subrahmanium, P.V. 1953: Summary of papers on *Tribal Welfare Conference* at Lohardaga.

Saha, N. and Barkotky, M.D. 1969: *Banshidua - report on socio-economic survey of a Garo village* (mimeographed). Jorhat, Agro-Economic Research Centre.

Saha, N. and Buragohain, D.K. 1970: Colonization scheme of shifting cultivators in Tripura (an assessment). *Indian Journal of Agricultural Economics*, Bombay, Vol.XXV, No.3.

Saha, N. 1970: *Carrying capacity of shifting cultivation: A study of Assam Hills*; Jorhat, Agro-Economic Research Centre.

Sahay, B.N. 1964: A note on the Kukis of Manipur. *Vanyajati*, Vol.XII, No.4.

Saikia, P.D. 1968: *Changes in Mikir society - report on socio-economic survey of a Karbi village*. Jorhat, Agro-Economic Research

Centre.

——1976: A note on shifting cultivation in North-East India. Paper submitted for discussion in the *first meeting of the Shifting Cultivation Board* held at New.Delhi.

Sanganna, T. 1966-67: Tribal problems in Orissa. *Adibasi*, Bhubaneshwar, Vol.VIII, No.2.

Sarkar, J. 1977: An observation on some economic aspects of the tribes of Arunachal Pradesh. Paper presented in the *Workshop on Tribal Economy*: Anthropological Survey of India. Calcutta.

Sastry, S.S. 1977: Forest policy towards Tribals in Karnataka - a historical survey paper presented in the Workshop on tribal presented in the *Workshop on Tribal Economy*, Anthropological Survey of India, Calcutta.

Singh, I.P. 1970: Development of agriculture in Tribal areas. *Indian Journal of Agricultural Economics*, Vol.XXV, No.3.

Sinha, D. 1977: The economy of the Hill Kharia of Purulia. Paper presented in the *Workshop on Tribal Economy*. Anthropological Survey of India, Calcutta.

Sisodia, J.S. and others. 1970: Agricultural development in Tribal Madhya Pradesh. *Indian Journal of Agricultural Economics*, Bombay, Vol.XXV, No.3.

Spencer, J.E. 1966: *Shifting cultivation in South-Eastern Asia*, Berkeley and Los Angeles: University of California Press.

Subrahmanium, P.V. 1953: Summary of papers on *Tribal Welfare Conference* at Lohardaga.

Tyler, Stephen A. 1974: Fields are for planting: swidden agriculture among the Koyas of South India *Journal of the Indian Anthropological Society*, Calcutta, Vol.IX.No.I.

Thangam, E.S. 1982: *Shifting Cultivation Control Programme in Wanchos Area*. Intanagar: Forest Department.

Vidyarthi, L.P. 1963: *Maler: a study in nature-man-spirit Complex of a Hill tribe in Bihar*. Calcutta, Book Land.

—— 1975: The future of traditional primitive societies, a case study of an Indian shifting cultivation society. *The Eastern Anthropologist*, Lucknow, Vol. XXVIII, No. 4.

Wadia, F.K. 1980: *"Control of Shifting Cultivation in the North-Eastern Region."* In T. Mathew, ed., *Tribal Economy of North-Eastern Region*. Gauhati: Spectrum Publications.

INDEX